Make a 2D Arcade Game in a Weekend

With Unity

Jodessiah Sumpter

Apress®

Make a 2D Arcade Game in a Weekend: With Unity

ISBN-13 (pbk): 978-1-4842-1495-4

ISBN-13 (electronic): 978-1-4842-1494-7

Managing Director: Welmoed Spahr
Lead Editor: Ben Renow-Clarke
Technical Reviewer: Marc Schärer
Editorial Board: Steve Anglin, Pramila Balan, Louise Corrigan, James T. DeWolf,
    Jonathan Gennick, Robert Hutchinson, Celestin Suresh John, Michelle Lowman,
    James Markham, Susan McDermott, Matthew Moodie, Jeffrey Pepper, Douglas Pundick,
    Ben Renow-Clarke, Gwenan Spearing
Coordinating Editor: Mark Powers
Copy Editor: Karen Jameson
Compositor: SPi Global
Indexer: SPi Global
Artist: SPi Global

Distributed to the book trade worldwide by Springer Science+Business Media New York, 233 Spring Street, 6th Floor, New York, NY 10013. Phone 1-800-SPRINGER, fax (201) 348-4505, e-mail orders-ny@springer-sbm.com, or visit www.springeronline.com. Apress Media, LLC is a California LLC and the sole member (owner) is Springer Science + Business Media Finance Inc (SSBM Finance Inc). SSBM Finance Inc is a Delaware corporation.

For information on translations, please e-mail rights@apress.com, or visit www.apress.com.

Apress and friends of ED books may be purchased in bulk for academic, corporate, or promotional use. eBook versions and licenses are also available for most titles. For more information, reference our Special Bulk Sales–eBook Licensing web page at www.apress.com/bulk-sales.

Any source code or other supplementary materials referenced by the author in this text is available to readers at www.apress.com/9781484214954. For detailed information about how to locate your book's source code, go to www.apress.com/source-code/. Readers can also access source code at SpringerLink in the Supplementary Material section for each chapter.

Contents at a Glance

About the Author ix

About the Technical Reviewer xi

Acknowledgments xiii

Introduction xv

■Chapter 1: Getting Started 1

■Chapter 2: Define Game Layout and Environment 23

■Chapter 3: Create Positioning and Movement 41

■Chapter 4: Scripting a Game Manager 61

■Chapter 5: Adding Sound and Music 83

■Chapter 6: Game Power-Ups 97

■Chapter 7: Level Manager and Menu 115

■Chapter 8: Publishing to the App Store 139

Index 157

Contents

About the Author ix

About the Technical Reviewer xi

Acknowledgments xiii

Introduction xv

■Chapter 1: Getting Started 1

Prerequisites 1

Install Unity 2

    Choosing a License... 4

    Welcome to Unity... 6

    Configuring Unity... 8

Skinning the Interface 10

    Learning the Views.. 11

    Understanding Layouts.. 16

Development Tips and Tricks... 18

    Changing Runtime Background Color.. 18

    Useful Hotkeys.. 20

Summary... 21

■Chapter 2: Define Game Layout and Environment 23

2D Game Design Setup.. 23

Laying Out the Game 25

Importing Assets 26

Define Screen Resolution 28

Adding Background 29

Adjusting Our Camera 32

Adding Bricks 32

    Creating PreFabs 33

    Creating Row of Bricks 35

    Add the Paddle 36

Add the Ball 38

Summary 39

■Chapter 3: Create Positioning and Movement 41

Making Our Ball Move 41

Handling Ball Collisions 44

Making Our Ball Bounce 46

Beginning Scripting 47

    The Rules of C Sharp (C#) 48

    Selecting an Editor 48

    Our First Script 48

    Moving the Paddle with the Mouse 52

    Launching the Ball with the Mouse 54

    Destroy the Blocks on Hit 57

Summary 60

■Chapter 4: Scripting a Game Manager 61

Keeping Our Ball in the Game Space 61

Creating Invisible Collider Walls 62

Changing the Impact of Gravity 64

Relabeling the Game Objects in Our Scene 66

Scripting Our Game Manager 67

Scripting Our Lose Collider..71

Using UI Text to Display Information..75

Summary...82

■Chapter 5: Adding Sound and Music......................................83

Adding Background Music...83

Adding Start and End Sounds..85

Bricks with Action and Impact Sound...86

Modify Brick Script for Sound..87

Game Area Sounds for the Walls and Paddle..................................92

Summary...95

■Chapter 6: Game Power-Ups...97

Building Power-Up Scripts..97

Building Base Power-Up Prefab Scripts..99

Extra Balls Script...100

Change Paddle Size Script...105

Creating Prefab Game Objects for Ball and Paddle Changes..............106

Sprites for Prefabs...107

Extra Ball Prefab..107

Shrink and Grow Prefabs..108

Putting it All Together in the Scene...111

Modify the Lose Script...113

Summary...114

■Chapter 7: Level Manager and Menu...................................115

Creating Intro Scene..115

Add a Main Title and Buttons..115

Script for Loading a Level...118

Modifying the Game Lose Scenario...121

Add Restart and Main Menu Buttons..121

Add a Panel for the Buttons...121

Updating the GameManager and Lose Scripts 122

Rename and Duplicate Main Scene 128

Modifying Level 1 to Include Level Manager......................................128

Adding Scenes to the Build Settings 130

Add Additional Buttons 131

Background Music 134

Trailing Ball Effect 134

Summary...137

■Chapter 8: Publishing to the App Store 139

Investigating Deployment Options..139

Defining Build Settings...140

Adding a Quit Button...144

Button Creation and LevelLoader Script Modification 145

Deploying to WebGL 146

Unity Cloud Build...148

Placing Our Game in GitHub 149

Adding your GitHub to the Cloud...152

Summary...155

Index...157

About the Author

Jodessiah Sumpter currently is the Chief Technology Officer for numerous start-up companies including Perfomatix Innovations and Food Cowboy. He has over 10 years of software development experience at Fortune 500 companies and has 20+ years experience developing websites and Internet marketing materials for individuals, non-profits, start-ups and small businesses.

Joe has also developed and deployed numerous mobile and TV applications for Android, iOS, Blackberry, Windows, and Samsung Smart TV. His company Blue Crystal Web Design has won numerous awards with the most recent being the AT&T U-Verse Hackathon and the Extreme Reality Android Challenge.

Joe is a serial entrepreneur who specializes in taking the software ideas of his national clients from concept to reality. He received an MBA from the University of Buffalo and a Post Masters degree in Marketing from the University of Dayton. You can reach find him on Twitter @bcwdesign or view his blog at http://www.bluecrystalwebdesign.com.

About the Technical Reviewer

Marc Schärer is an interactive media software engineer and contributor to the Unity forums as a fulltime professional unity user since 2007–2008. As a Swiss local, he attempts to support the local development communities in Switzerland to help them unleash their potential, applying his experience delivering interactive 3d learning, training and entertainment experiences to mobile, desktop and web platforms for customers around the world.

He has a strong background in the 3D graphics, network technology, software engineering and interactive media fields, which first interested him as a teenager. He studied Computer Science and Computational Science and Engineering at the Swiss Federal Institute of Technology in Zürich.

He is currently the Chief VR Officer at vantage.tv, a company he co-founded in 2014, which seeks to revolutionize how we see and experience events of any type and scale in the future by removing the barrier of distance.

Acknowledgments

First I would like to give glory to God. This book would not have been written if this skinny, anxious, and shy kid from the ghetto didn't believe that he could accomplish anything through Him. Thank you to my amazing wife Cunard for all of her love, support and patience during this book writing process. I must also thank my wonderful kids Jayden and Angel. Papa would not have accomplished this book without your hugs, kisses, jokes and smiles whenever I needed a break or distraction. You are my heart.

Thank you to my family and friends for all of their support and words of encouragement while writing this book. Especially to my Mom who has always pushed me to be better and my brother Jeremiah who created the music for the book. The beats take this book and my games to another level so thanks so much for being there for me bro.

Last and definitely not least I want to thank the outstanding team at Apress. Thanks to Steve Anglin for being my first contact many years ago and starting me on the book writing journey. Thank you to my editors Mark Powers and Ben Renow-Clarke for giving me the continuous poking and prodding I needed to get the job done. You guys were a great support and I appreciate your patience and understanding during the process. A special thanks to my technical reviewer Marc Schärer as well for making sure I had my stuff together and for encouraging thoughts for each chapter.

Introduction

Mobile games are among the most popular types of apps that mobile device owner's use. According to App Annie, mobile games hold 7 of the top 10 grossing apps for 2015 at the time of this writing. With the introduction of game development platforms like Unity, GameSalad and Corona, the ability to build a complete highly engaging game has become easier to create. Anyone with basic programming and game design understanding can build and release a game for the masses to enjoy.

What is the Book About

In this book we use the Unity software to build a simple brick breaker game. A brick breaker game allows the player to eliminate bricks on the screen by hitting them with a ball. The player uses the paddle to keep the ball in the game and loses if the ball passes the paddle.

We will walk through using Unity to rebuild this classic game. We will learn how to add simple graphics and sounds to make the game interactive. In addition we will use the Unity editor and the Unity Cloud to build the game for web, mobile and WebGL.

Who is the Book For

This book was written for the Unity 3D beginner. It does assume that you are familiar with working with a computer and comfortable with understanding basic programming. Other than that no experience with the Unity software is expected. Familiarity with the old Atari Super Breakout game play is helpful as well so you can understand the logic of the basic game we will create.

How To Contact Me

I would love to hear from you! You can contact me as well as get updated information on the book here:

Joe Sumpter
Twitter: @bcwsdesign
Site: http://www.breakthosebricks.com
Email: joe@breakthosebricks.com

Unity is updated all the time so I would suggest signing up for the email list on the site or visiting the Errata section for the book on the Apress site for the latest information on the book.

CHAPTER 1

■ ■ ■

Getting Started

Unity is a development framework for creating 2D and 3D games. With this framework, you can create interactive content for a multitude of platforms including the desktop, mobile devices, and gaming consoles. The latest version of Unity supports development for iOS, Android, Windows, Blackberry 10, OS X, Linux, Internet browsers, PlayStation, Xbox, and Wii U.

The primary focus of this chapter is to walk through the setup and installation of Unity and provide the basic information on laying out a project in Unity. You will learn the system requirements as well as the licensing details for choosing the Unity version to use.

This book will walk through the latest version of Unity today, which is Unity 5.1.2. Unity is constantly being updated, and version 5, the latest major release, was delivered in early 2015.

Let's get started!

■ **Note**   The primary focus of this book will be development on a MacBook Pro. If you plan to develop for a PC, please visit the site notes online at http://www.apress.com/9781484214954.

Prerequisites

In order to begin learning how to use Unity, you need to confirm that you have the right computer equipment to run the software. Unity is a powerful editor and 3D engine that requires your computer to have enough horsepower to utilize the product effectively.

First you should verify that your system supports the general requirements for Unity development (see Figure 1-1).

FOR DEVELOPMENT

OS: Windows XP SP2+, 7 SP1+, 8; Mac OS X 10.8+.

Windows Vista is not supported; and server versions of Windows & OS X are not tested.

GPU: Graphics card with DX9 (shader model 2.0) capabilities. Anything made since 2004 should work.

The rest mostly depends on the complexity of your projects.

Additional platform development requirements:

- iOS: Mac computer running minimum OS X 10.9.4 version and Xcode 6.x.
- Android: Android SDK and Java Development Kit (JDK).
- Windows 8/8.1 Store Apps / Windows Phone 8/8.1: 64 bit Windows 8.1 Pro and Visual Studio 2013 Update 2+.
- Blackberry: 32 bit Java Runtime (JRE).
- WebGL: Mac OS X 10.8+ or Windows 7 SP1+ (64-bit editor only)

Figure 1-1. *System Requirements for installing the Unity software from Unity3d.com*

After you have verified your computer hardware and software are supported, let's install the Unity software.

Install Unity

Download and run the installer for Unity on your system. The system used for development for this book is a MacBook Pro running the Lion operating system. However, as Figure 1-1 indicated, you can develop using Unity on both Windows and Mac PCs. After downloading and double-clicking the file for the Mac, you will see the Download Assistant window shown in Figure 1-2. The assistant window provides the release notes for the version of Unity that you are trying to install and the ability to begin the software installation.

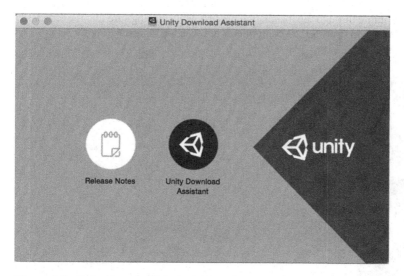

Figure 1-2. Unity Download Assistant

Next you will double-click on the Download Assistant icon to begin the installation (shown in Figure 1-3).

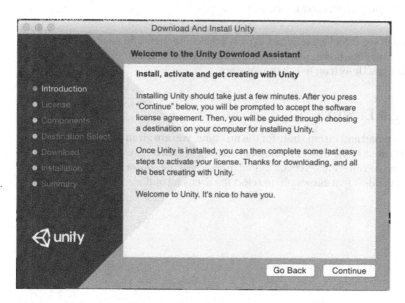

Figure 1-3. Download introduction window for Unity

Click to continue through the installation process while making sure that the Standard Assets, Web Player, and Unity 5.1.2f1 components are selected for install (Figure 1-4).

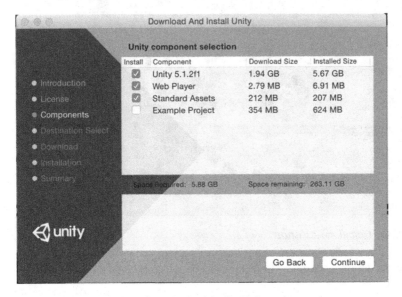

Figure 1-4. *Component selection window for Unity*

You also will see the space required to install the components on your system. Once the installation has completed, you can start using the Unity software. You simply have to double-click on the Unity icon to run the software.

Choosing a License

When you download and install Unity for the first time, you are given the option to install a 30-day trial license of the Unity Professional version. This license will allow you to test out the features of Professional version before investing in the software. Figure 1-5 shows the Activation window that allows you to select the licensing options available.

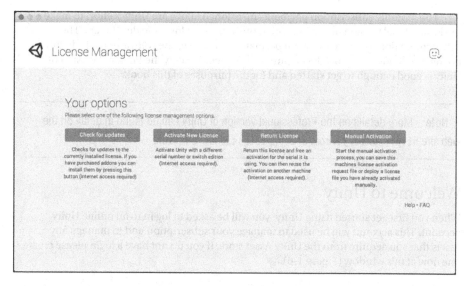

Figure 1-5. *License selection window for Unity*

The Professional version of the software offers numerous advantages primarily centered around the needs of a professional Unity game developer. For example, the Professional version of Unity will allow you to use game performance reporting to analyze managed code crashes, change your editor skin from gray to black, and customize your splash screen. In addition you will get access to 12 free months of Unity Cloud Build Pro. We will use Unity Cloud in Chapter 8 to build our simple game online. If you would like to review the differences between the Unity Personal (free) and the Unity Professional version, you can find that on the Unity webs site at:

```
http://unity3d.com/get-unity
```

In addition you can review the licensing information to ensure you qualify to release games under the Personal license here at:

```
http://unity3d.com/legal/eula
```

The Professional version of the software currently costs $1500 or $75 a month for the base platform. Each mobile and console device platform export is considered to be an add-on to the Unity base package. Each add-on has its own individual deployment pricing in addition to the base platform cost. Also the Android, Blackberry, Windows, and iOS add-on packages for Unity have Personal and Professional versions. For example, the Personal Android add-on for Unity is free for Indie developers making less than $100,000 in annual revenue or by an educational, academic, nonprofit, or government entity with a total annual budget for the entire entity (based on prior fiscal year) in excess of US$100,000. As with the base Unity software, the Professional version of the Android add-on is an additional $1500 or $75 a month. Therefore the total cost for obtaining the Professional version of Unity for Android development is $3000 or $150 a month.

The monthly subscription payments mentioned above are Unity's effort to make the Professional version of the software more affordable for Indie developers. The subscription does not give you a full permanent license to the software so it is definitely not recommended for most development shops. Fortunately the Personal version of Unity is good enough to get started and for the purposes of this book.

■ **Note**   More details on the Professional version of Unity can be found in detail on the web site http://unity3d.com/unity/professional-edition.

Welcome to Unity

When you first get started using Unity, you will be asked to log in to an online Unity account. This account will be used to manage your subscription and to manage any assets that you acquire from the Unity Asset store. If you do not have a login please create one now at this window (Figure 1-6).

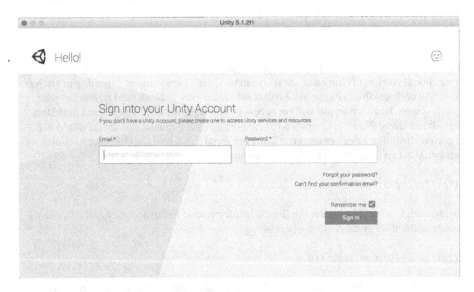

Figure 1-6. *Sign-In window for Unity Account*

Once you are signed in, you will be provided the option to enter your subscription serial number for the Professional version or to choose the Unity Personal Edition (Figure 1-7).

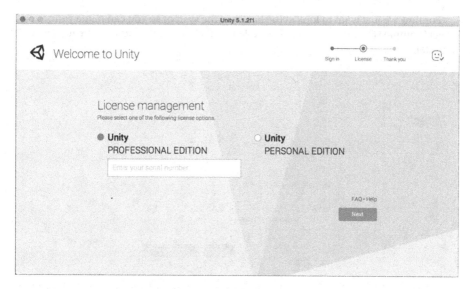

Figure 1-7. License management window for Unity Account

Next you will see the Projects window (Figure 1-8) where you can either choose the project you will open of create a new project to begin. Select "New Project" located at the top right of the window so we can create our 2D project (Figure 1-9).

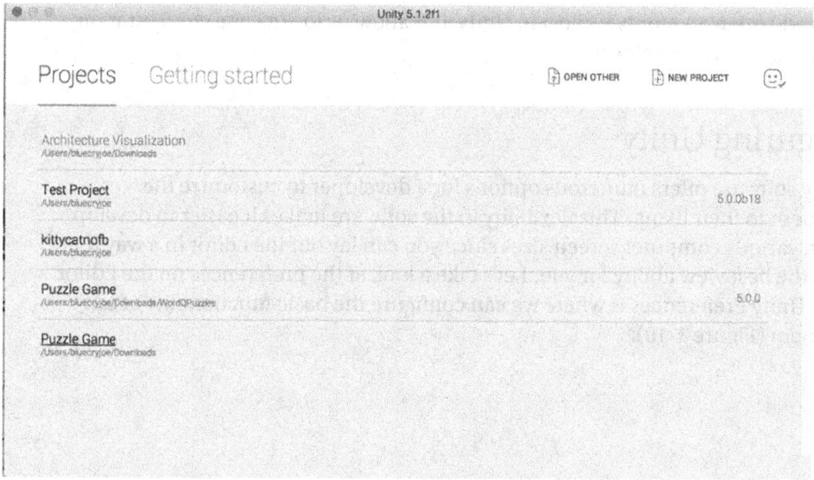

Figure 1-8. Projects window for new or existing projects

7

For now we just want to look at the basics of the system so you can name your project "Sample Unity Project" (see Figure 1-9) and choose a location to save it on your computer.

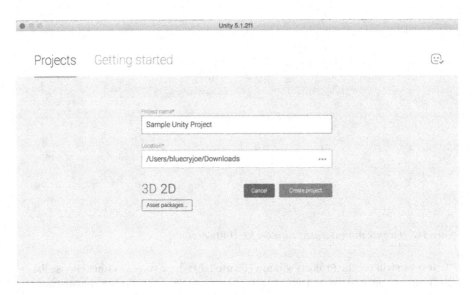

Figure 1-9. *New project window with 2D and 3D options*

This will open an empty project in Unity and allow us to view the configuration options available in the software.

Configuring Unity

The Unity software offers numerous options for a developer to customize the environment to their liking. This flexibility in the software makes it easier to develop games on various computer screen sizes since you can lay out the editor in a way that provides the best view ability for you. Let's take a look at the preferences on the Editor first. The Unity Preferences is where we can configure the basic functionality of our environment (Figure 1-10).

Figure 1-10. *Empty Project for Unity*

Click on the word "Unity" located at the top left-hand corner of the application window.

Select the Preferences option (or select and hold command button and press comma) to open the Unity Preferences window. There are numerous options here that we can modify to customize our Editor to our liking. Go ahead and select the External Tools option from the menu on the left-hand side. Here you will find the External Script Editor. MonoDevelop is the IDE supplied with Unity and should be the default. If it is not selected, please change the editor to MonoDevelop Figure 1-11).

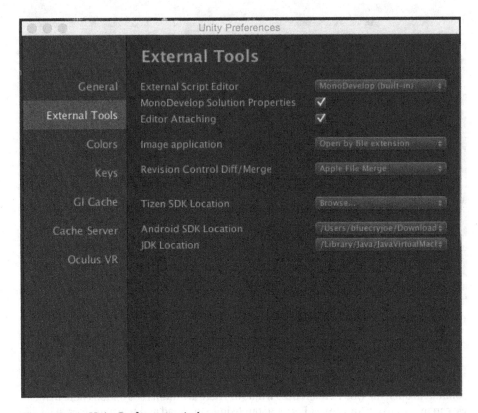

Figure 1-11. *Unity Preferences window*

Next we will learn how to modify our interface look. The next section will only matter if you are using the 30-day trial or have paid for the Professional version of the software. Feel free to skip the section if you are only developing with the Personal version of Unity.

Skinning the Interface

There are two skins for Unity: the dark (black) skin and the light (gray) one. The Personal (i.e., free) version of Unity only allows for you to choose the gray skin as the color of the interface. Once you upgrade to the Professional license, you get the option to choose between the two skin colors. The option to choose between the skins is located in the preferences options found by selecting Unity, Preferences, and then selecting General in the left navigation (see Figure 1-12).

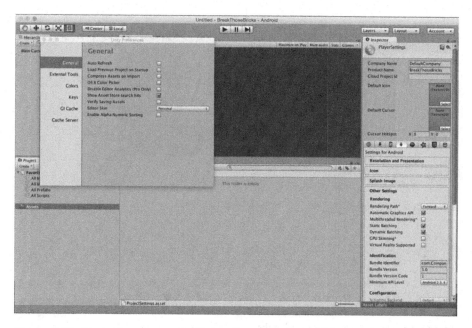

Figure 1-12.   *General preferences for Unity. Choose the drop-down next to Skin (Pro Only) to toggle between the different types*

Since we are trying to limit our costs for game development, we will use the Personal version of Unity for this book. We will leave the other options at the defaults for now. Close the Unity Preferences window.

Learning the Views

The next thing we want to do is to lay out the various windows of the Unity interface in a way that makes it easier for us to build our 2D game. These windows in the Editor are called views, and the main ones we will use are the following six (see Figure 1-13):

- Project View

- Hierarchy View

- Scene View

- Game View

- Inspector View

- Console

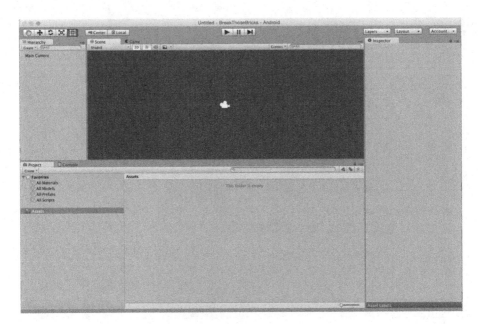

Figure 1-13. *Display of the available tabs*

■ **Note**   There are actually four additional views.

The Project View, shown in Figure 1-14, displays the assets that are part of your project. These assets include all materials, models, prefabs, and scripts.

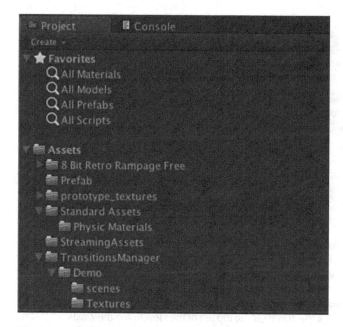

Figure 1-14. Example of Project View details

The Project View also allows you to view assets in the store directly without opening the Asset Store window. For example, if you select All Models in the Project View, you will see a list of any models you have imported in the asset view on the right. If you want to view available assets in the Asset Store, simply select the Asset Store option from the Search option bar (see Figure 1-15). This will display both the Free and the Paid assets that you can use within your projects.

Figure 1-15. Embedded asset store with Model option selected in Project View

Hierarchy View displays all of the GameObjects that are included in the current Scene. The default project starts with only a Main Camera object. If you double-click the GameObject in the Hierarchy View, the focus will shift to the object in the Scene View (see Figure 1-16).

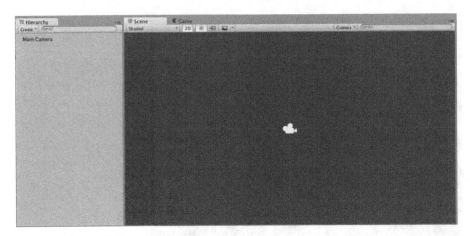

Figure 1-16. Default Hierarchy and Scene View

The Scene View displays the layout of the scene. You use this view to move objects around and lay them out for your game. The GameObjects can be moved on their X, Y, Z axes using the red, green, and blue arrows that appear in the Scene View. Since we are creating a 2D game, you will need to click the 2D text at the top left of the view to see the Z axis.

The Game View, shown in Figure 1-17, shows how the GameObjects will display when the game is played. If you switch to this view without pressing the play button on the Toolbar, the game will display at a standstill. Pressing the play button will automatically switch to this view and execute the scene you are working on.

Figure 1-17. A basic project with only the camera view will show an empty blue screen when the game is played

The Inspector View (Figure 1-18) displays all the attributes and parameters of any selected GameObjects. In addition you can use it to view Unity settings and review selected scripts and components.

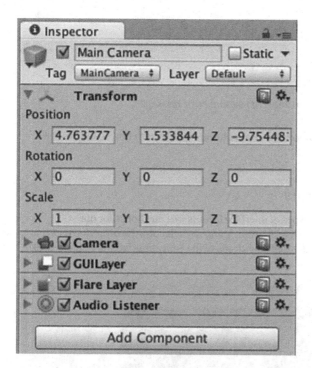

Figure 1-18. *Inspector View of the Main Camera object*

The Console displays any output written to the log from scripts, warning messages, or error messages from your game. For error messages outputted from your scripts, you can double-click them to be taken to the section that the error occurred. As you see in Figure 1-19 there are four different options in the Console View.

- Clear – Will remove all messages written to the Console

- Collapse – This can be enabled or disabled. When enabled it allows duplicate messages to only be displayed once.

- Clear on Play – This can be enabled or disabled. When enabled this will clear the console once the Play mode is entered.

- Error Pause - This can be enabled or disabled. When enabled this will pause the game when Debug.LogError() is called in your script.

15

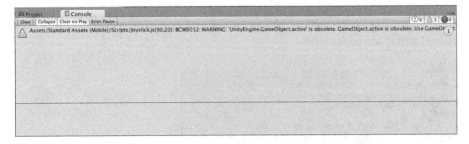

Figure 1-19. *Console View with example of random error message*

Now that we have learned about the available views, let's learn how to lay out the views in a custom way.

Understanding Layouts

There are five different included types of interface layouts we can choose for our development environment. You will review the options by selecting the drop-down next to the Layers drop-down on the upper right-hand side of the Unity interface (see Figure 1-20).

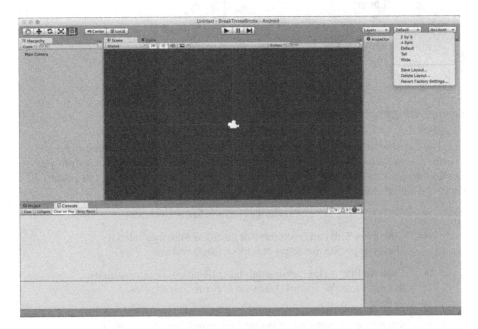

Figure 1-20. *Shows list of default layout view options*

- The 2 x 3 layout enlarges the Scene and the Game views on the left-hand side of your screen. The middle section contains your objects in the Hierarchy View, and the right side contains the Project and Inspector Views.

- The 4 Split layout gives you four view different angles of our Scene at different points of the X, Y, and Z axes. The middle section has the Hierarchy and Project Views, and the right side contains the Inspector View.

- The Default layout places the Hierarchy and Scene/Game Views at the top of the interface. The Project and the Console Views are laid at the bottom of the screen.

- The Tall layout enlarges the Scene/Game Views on the right-hand side, places the Hierarchy and Project Views in the middle section, and the Inspector on the right-hand side.

- The Wide view places the Scene/Game Views at the top half of the interface in a large wide format. At the bottom of the interface, the Hierarchy View is to the left and the Project View to the right. On the far right of the screen is the Inspector View.

You can also create a Custom Layout based on the way you would like the interface to look. Figure 1-21 shows the option to save and create a custom name for a layout. We can add or remove windows, expand or contract areas, etc.

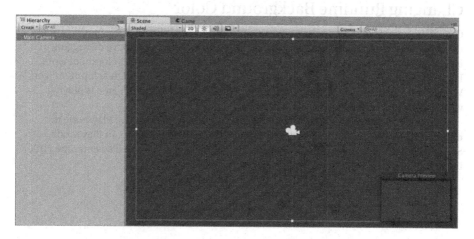

Figure 1-21. *Hierarchy View displaying the Main Camera selected*

The Scene View shows the current scene you are working on. When you start a new project, the only object in the Scene View is the Main Camera. You can find and highlight the Main Camera in your scene, as in Figure 1-21, by double-clicking on the Main Camera in the Hierarchy View.

The Main Camera will be used to display the areas that we want our user to view. We will need to position or move the camera around our GameObjects in order for them to be visible in our game.

■ **Note**   You can choose to have multiple cameras in a scene for a 3D game but we can keep it simple and use one camera for our 2D creation.

Ok, we should have a basic understanding of our views and how to lay them out. Let's look at a few tips and tricks we can use as well create our game to speed up development.

Development Tips and Tricks

When working as a developer, any setting, action, or repeatable process that saves you time or improves productivity is extremely beneficial. In this section we will look at some of the shortcuts we will use throughout the book as we create our game. I encourage you to look at the drop-down menu and the Unity documentation to find additional shortcuts that will help your development efforts. OK, let's begin with modification of our Editor color when our game is running.

Changing Runtime Background Color

One of the great things about development in Unity is the ability to make modifications to you game and see the results in real time. This allows for very effective debugging of issues and lets you to alter your game experience while doing your development work. However while this is a great feature of Unity, it does offer risks of lost development work. We can reduce this risk by setting a different runtime color when our game is playing within our user preferences.

Figure 1-22 shows our options when we have color definition. The Playmode tint option is what we want to set in order to change the color when we are in Play mode. Select the color next to the text and choose a light blue color. You can also enter the HEX information for the color that I used as 6CE2F9FF.

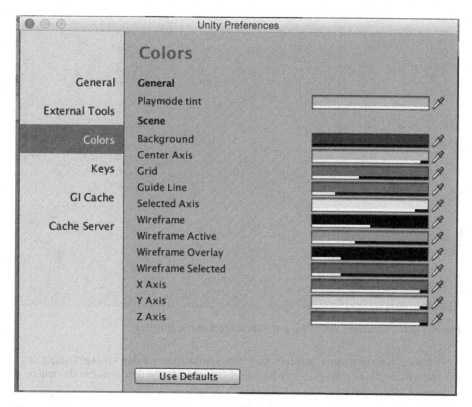

Figure 1-22. Unity Preferences screen with Color option selected

You can see the results of this change by pressing the Play button in the middle of the Unity screen. Your screen should now look like Figure 1-23 and have a blue tint covering the entire Editor.

Figure 1-23. *Play screen with Blue tint indicating that it is running*

This will help us determine when the game is running so we don't make changes to our game while it is in a run state. We have nothing in our scene right now but this will be very useful later. Trust me.

Useful Hotkeys

Using shortcuts and hotkeys can help reduce the amount of time it takes for you to develop your next great game. Table 2-1 shows a few keyboard hotkeys that can help you use Unity more efficiently.

Table 2-1. *List of useful Unity commands*

Key	Command
Q	Activates the Pan option in the toolbar
W	Activates the move toolbar
E	Activates the Rotate toolbar option
R	Activates the scale toolbar option for resizing objects
T	Activates the Rect Tool

Figure 1-24 shows the keys that the hotkeys refer to. These keys are located at the top left of the screen above the Hierarchy View. We will use these hotkeys through the book as we build and navigate the project and scenes.

***Figure 1-24.** Unity editor tools*

■ **Note**   Additional hotkey information can be found on the Unity site here:
http://docs.unity3d.com/Documentation/Manual/UnityHotkeys.html.

Summary

In this chapter we discussed the system requirements and additional software need for developing with the Unity software. We walked through the different Views that are part of the Unity Editor as well as the different layouts that are available in the system. In addition we discussed some of the developer shortcuts that are available to make your life easier.

In the next chapter we will discuss setting up the project for our game and begin building the basic structure of the gameplay.

> *The secret of getting ahead is getting started. The secret of getting started is breaking your complex overwhelming tasks into small manageable tasks, and starting on the first one.*

—Mark Twain

■ ■ ■

CHAPTER 2

Define Game Layout and Environment

As mentioned earlier in this book, Unity can be used for both 3D and 2D game development. The thought process for laying out a 2D game is very different than a 3D game in Unity since the environmental options and tools used are specific to each game type. Two-dimensional game development typically involves simpler graphics and design process using assets that are limited to a horizontal and vertical plane.

In Chapter 2 we will learn about the various layout options that Unity provides for developers to tailor their environment preferences. Also we will configure these environmental preferences in a way that works for 2D game development.

Let's begin talking about 2D!

■ **Note** For more information and tutorials on 2D Game Development in Unity, please refer to the Unity 2D Game Creation web site at `https://unity3d.com/learn/tutorials/topics/2d-game-creation`.

2D Game Design Setup

Building a 2D game in Unity is very different from building a 3D game. Unity provides individualized tools and settings that are tailored toward each game type and assist the game developer in having the right environment for game creation. In Chapter 1 when we defined our Project, we choose 2D as the development type for our game (Figure 1-9). At this point we will repeat the process we used and create a new game project called "Break Those Bricks." Again we will set the project type to 2D (Figure 2-1) as we create it and leave the default asset packages defined.

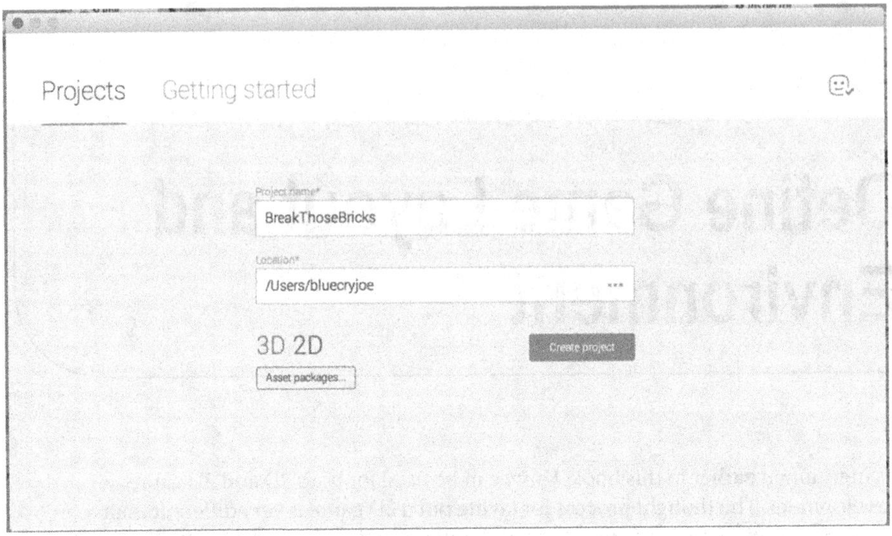

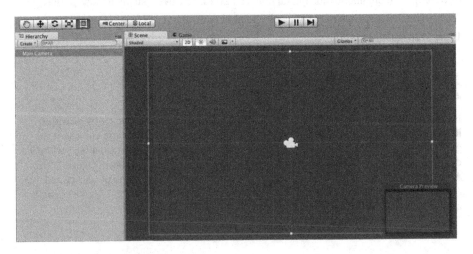

Figure 2-1. *Defining the project name and type*

By choosing the 2D project type, we instruct Unity to define the preferences in the software to support effective 2D application development. This will set our Scene View into 2D mode, define the Default Behavior of our Editor to 2D, and set our main camera to Orthographic mode. Figure 2-2 shows what the Scene View looks like for the 2D mode. The Rect Tool (HotKey T) is selected, and the Main Camera object is the only thing that is set in our scene.

Figure 2-2. *Scene View with 2D*

Next let's set the layout we will work into for the Unity Editor. To make it easier for us to view the game as we develop our scenes, we will switch the layout to 2 x 3. This is accomplished by selecting this option from the second drop-down on the top right of the Unity Editor interface. Then within the Project View, let's create three folders for us to hold our main project assets. The folder names are Scenes, Sprites, and Scripts. They can be created by right-clicking on the Assets folder name in the Project View and then selecting Create, then Folder.

Once the folders are created, our screen should look like Figure 2-3. We can then begin thinking about the layout of our game and what the user experience will be.

Figure 2-3. Assets folder with three created folders

Laying Out the Game

The goal of our project is to build a 2D Brick Breaker game. Our game will be similar to the classic games Super Breakout and Arkanoid by Atari and Taito that were really popular back in the 1980s. The game elements were really simple and include a Paddle, Ball, and Blocks (i.e., Bricks) displayed on the screen. We will also include enhancements like power-ups and music to improve our user experience. The goal for the user playing the classic games was to eliminate the Blocks on the screen by hitting the ball into them. Our game player would accomplish this by using the Paddle to ensure that the ball did not fall off the bottom of the screen. Figure 2-4 shows an example of the typical layout for a classic brick breaker game.

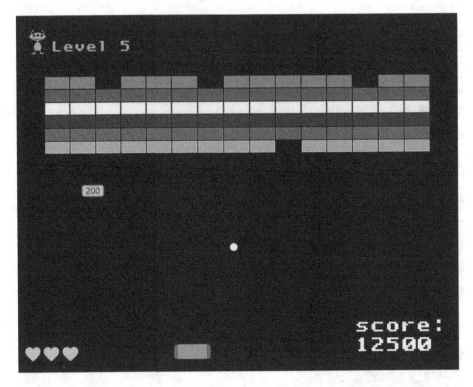

Figure 2-4. *Sample of a classic brick breaker game layout*

Some of the Blocks would provide bonus features (i.e., power-ups) that would be released when the ball hit it and which had to be caught by the Paddle. These items would either have positive or negative consequences to the player and potentially would impact the game play. In addition they could provide additional balls that will help eliminate the blocks faster. We will follow the basic outline of these classic games for our creation while adding our own unique aspects to the design.

Importing Assets

Since we have our folders laid out within our Asset folder, we can begin importing the game assets we will need to build our 2D game. The items we will need to get started are our graphics for the background and the game objects used as part of the game play. These items will be imported as Sprites without any depth since this is a 2D game. A Sprite is simply a compute graphic that can be moved onscreen. Unity provides a built-in Sprite Editor and also includes some really cool features for Sprite manipulation and management. We will discuss these features later in the book as we build our game.

For now we will begin by importing the Sprites into our project. The items that we need are included with the book and are called background.png, ball.gif, greenbrick. gif, and paddle.gif. This can be done by opening the folder where these Sprites are located and dragging them into the Unity Editor onto the Sprites folder. This will place the files in that folder in our project. Figure 2-5 shows how our Project View looks with the images included.

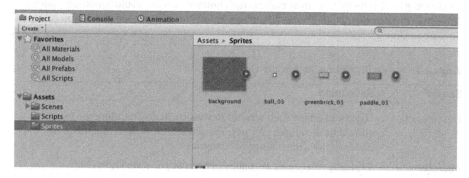

Figure 2-5. *Imported Sprites*

If you select the greenbrick.gif and look at the Inspector View on the right in the Unity Editor, you will see details on the imported Sprite. There is also a button for access to the Sprite editor listed that we will dive into that later in the chapter.

Now that we have our basic asset import completed, let's go ahead and save our scene. This can be accomplished by selecting File and then Save Scene from the main Unity menu. We will name the scene as "Main" and save it to the default Assets folder. Once the save is done, navigate to the Assets folder in the project view and drag and drop the Main scene in the Scenes folder.

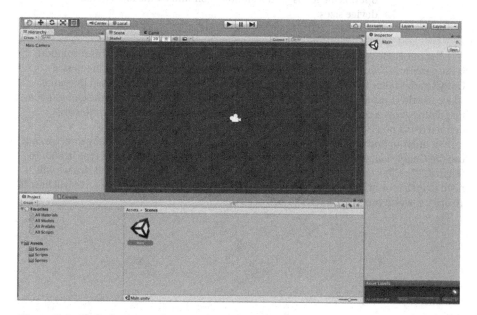

Figure 2-6. *Main Scene saved in our Assets/Scene folder*

Define Screen Resolution

With the various device types and screen sizes you can develop for in Unity, one of the challenging decisions that we must make is the choice of screen resolution to develop for. Table 2-1 contains the details on the screen resolutions for the types of games you can develop in Unity.

Table 2-1. *Screen Resolution Suggestions By Device*

Screen	Resolution
Desktop/PC	Users can adjust their screens to various sizes. Therefore the focus should be developing for popular screen resolutions that meet the needs of the widest range of customers.
Microconsole	Typically run games at 1080p (1920x1080) or 720p (1280x720)
iOS	Have various resolutions depending on the generation of device. These include: - 960x640px (iPhone 4) - 1136x640px (iPhone 5) - 1024x768px (iPad 1st gen, iPad 2, iPad Mini), - 2048x1536px (iPad 3rd gen, iPad 4th gen, iPad Air, iPad mini 2nd gen), - 2732-by-2048 (iPad Pro)
Android	There are tons of Android devices available with dozens of screen resolutions attributed to them. Since there are so many resolution options the focus for development should be the most popular device sizes.

For our game we are going to focus on the resolution of 800x600px. This resolution is the generic 4:3 resolution that is popular for many mobile and desktop screen sizes. Unity's game space is actually defined by Unity World Units and not pixels in the game space. World Units are the position in the Transform (in the Inspector) of the game space that defines how a certain image will be displayed. The sizes of unscaled sprites are defined using pixels to units by Unity.

In order to find out the pixel size and number of bricks we need for our game, we can use the Google calculator. Just navigate to Google.com in any browser and type in 800/10 (Figure 2-7). Click enter and you will get the response of 80. This is the pixel size we will need to great our bricks and represent the World Unit size of our brick asset. We will have 10 brick rows on our scene each at a size of 80 pixels.

Figure 2-7. Google calculator from main page

Now that we have a plan for our screen size and brick assets, let's begin building by starting with adding a background image to our game.

Adding Background

The background of our game is what adds the coolness and unique feel for our game player. The classic Arkanoid game used a very generic blue background that had some simple texture to it. For our project we will start with the background.png file that we imported into our Sprites folder earlier in the chapter (Figure 2-8). Let's drag the background image to the Main scene by placing it in our Hierarchy View.

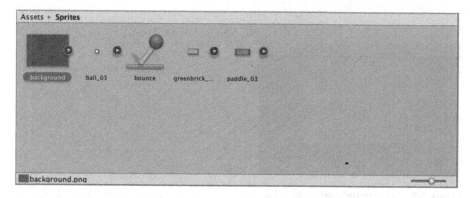

Figure 2-8. Background sprite

If we select the background image and look at the Inspector (Figure 2-9), we will see the details on the Sprite with an option to view the Sprite Editor. The Sprite Editor allows us to modify our image and set the necessary parameters for defining the location of the background within our screen resolution. Since we only need one image for our background, our Sprite Mode is set to Single. If our Sprite texture contains multiple images to be used in our project, we would set the mode to multiple to handle extraction of each image.

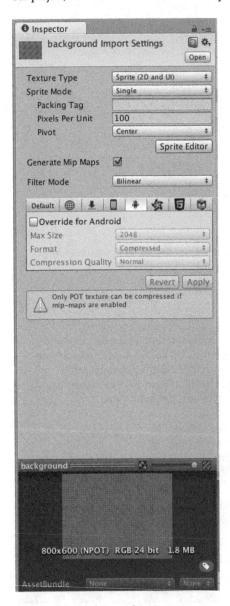

Figure 2-9. Background Sprite Inspector

Now we will set the Pivot point of our background from the center to the bottom left. You can accomplish this by either choosing bottom left next the Pivot in the Inspector or by editing the location by opening the Sprite Editor. Figure 2-10 shows the Sprite Editor with the point at the bottom left corner of the background image. This will allow us to work from left to right as we add assets to our game.

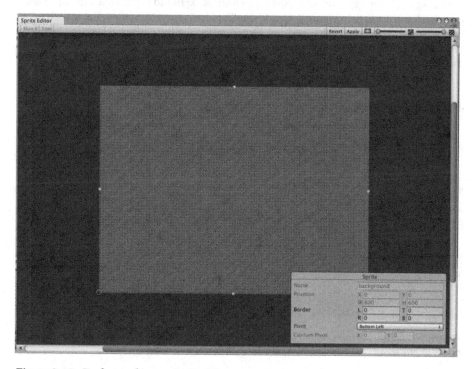

Figure 2-10. Backgound image Sprite Editor

Next add the background image to the scene by dragging and dropping the image under the Main Camera. Then set the Camera location from Center to Pivot by clicking button at the top middle (Figure 2-11).

Figure 2-11. Setting Pivot of Camera

This will ensure that our camera is fixed on the pivot area that we set for the background and not in the middle of our screen.

Adjusting Our Camera

With our Pivot set now, we can adjust our camera to cover the entire 4:3 background area. We want the people to play our game with the entire screen filled with the background image. Currently when we select the camera we will see the outline covering the center of our background image. In order to cover the entire background we will need to adjust the camera size to a size 6. In Figure 2-3 under the Camera Inspector is where the new size can be set. Once the size is changed, our camera will cover the entire background image. We can verify this by pressing the Play button in the middle of the screen and looking at the Game View. You will see the entire background screen displayed like in Figure 2-12.

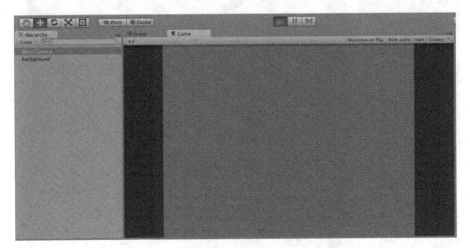

Figure 2-12. Play button selected and blank background shown. Let's now add some bricks to our scene

Adding Bricks

One of the core parts of our game are the bricks. Our bricks will be simple yet colorful and are one of the key components to the fun in our game. Our game will be different from the classic bricks game since we will not just list bricks across the entire screen. Instead we will strategically place the bricks in the scene and even eventually add some movement to them. To get started we need to add 13 bricks to our screen.

Creating PreFabs

When you want to create multiples of the same object in a game Scene, Unity offers an asset type called a PreFab. A PreFab allows you to store a GameObject with all of its attributes and properties. When you make changes to the PreFab object, it will change the properties of all of the objects created from it.

Since we have to create 13 bricks that will be mirrored within our Scene, we will start off by creating a PreFab. First drag our brick image named greenbrick.png from our Sprites folder (Figure 2-5) into our Scene. The brick will be placed on the lower left corner of our background image in our scene (Figure 2-13).

Figure 2-13. Green Brick added to the scene

Now select the brick to show the object Inspector. Let's change the Transform Position to X to 8 and Y to 6. Also let's change the X/Y of our Scale to the same numbers. We should now see our brick near the center of our screen. Now right-click on the Assets folder in your Project View, select Create and New Folder. Name the folder Prefab since we will use it to store the Prefab assets we create. Once all is done your screen should look like Figure 2-14.

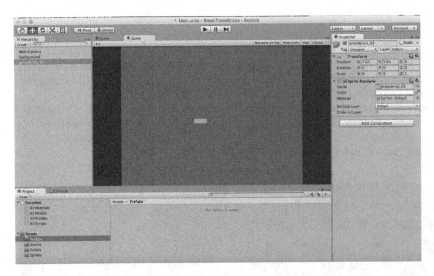

Figure 2-14. *Green Brick in the middle of the screen*

To create our Prefab for the brick we just drag the green brick object down unto the Prefab folder. You should now see the green brick in the folder and the name of the object should change from black text to blue text. Figure 2-15 shows how your view should look. We distinguish between our Prefab and regular assets in our screen by the color of the text and the description of the object in the Inspector window. Once you select the green brick object in the Hierarchy View, you should see Prefab listed with three interaction buttons (Select, Revert, Apply) in the Inspector window.

Figure 2-15. *Green brick prefab object*

Creating Row of Bricks

With our Prefab created we can now generate a row of bricks for our ball to eliminate. We will limit our first row to 13 bricks on our screen that will stretch horizontally across. It's really easy to create a new brick from our prefab using the duplicate feature in Unity. Simply right-click on the brick object in the Hierarchy View and select Duplicate. This will create a duplicate object with the same name of the object plus an incremental number in parentheses. We can also use the shortcut CMD+D on a Mac or CTRL+D on a Windows PC on a selected brick to create duplicates faster.

Go ahead and repeat this step 12 times so that there are 13 brick objects on the screen. Since we are creating duplicates, they will all be located in the same Transform location of our original object. We will need to select each object and move them to the appropriate locations on the screen.

Here are the Transform Position X coordinates to set in the Inspector for each object:

```
greenbrick_03: -7.4
greenbrick_03(1): -6.2
greenbrick_03(2): -5
greenbrick_03(3): -3.8
greenbrick_03(4): -2.6
greenbrick_03(5): -1.4
greenbrick_03(6): -0.2
greenbrick_03(7): 1
greenbrick_03(8): 2.2
greenbrick_03(9): 3.4
greenbrick_03(10): 4.6
greenbrick_03(11): 5.8
greenbrick_03(12): 7
```

If you notice, the spacing between each of the objects is 1.2. The Y and Z position attributes should be 0 for all objects as well. Once completed, Right-Click on an empty area of the Hierarchy Window and select Create Empty. This will create an empty game object that we can use to place our bricks under. This will allow us to coordinate and move the entire row of bricks together. Name the empty object Bricks for now. Select all of the brick objects that you created and drag them under the new Bricks game object. Your screen should now look like Figure 2-16.

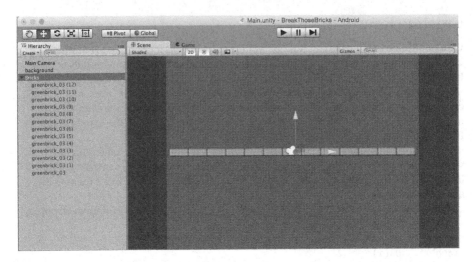

Figure 2-16. Row of green brick objects under Bricks game object

If your row of bricks is not centered like Figure 2-16 you will need to modify Transform of the Bricks object to have a Position of X:8.2 Y:6 Z:0. Your bricks should now be centered in your Scene View. Next we will add a Paddle to our scene.

■ **Note** Never played Super Breakout by Atari before? Well the Google Search engine provides a free way for you to play online through the browser. Simply visit http://google.com and search for "Atari Breakout." Click on Images and you will see a playable version of the game using random images. Pretty cool!

Add the Paddle

The Paddle is one of the main interactive objects that are included in our game. Users will either use their directional pads or touch to move it left or right on the screen. It will be used to prevent the ball from falling off the screen as well as to collect the power-ups that will fall from our bricks. Since we will only have one Paddle in our screen, we will not create a Prefab object for it. Instead we will have the one main object and modify it as needed.

1. To add the Paddle to our scene, go to the Sprites folder in the Project View and select the Paddle object.

2. Drag and drop the object in the Hierarchy View so that it appears in the scene at Position 0.

3. Modify the Transform Properties in the Inspector to match Figure 2-17, which includes the appropriate scale and positioning on the screen.

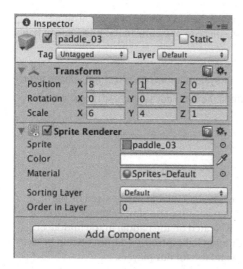

Figure 2-17. Inspector for our Paddle

The Paddle should now be located in the middle of our Game View beneath the bricks. If we click on it or try to move it using the directional keys on our keyboard, it will not move. We will need to add interactivity and movement in the next chapter.

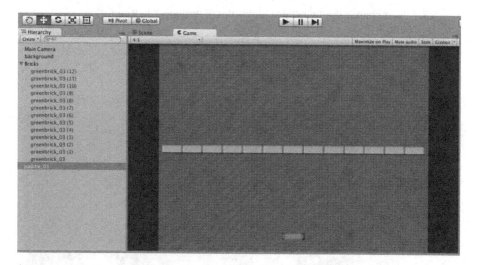

Figure 2-18. Game View with Paddle in position

Ok, as you see our game is really starting to take the basic shape of a typical Super Breakout or Arkanoid game. We have one last key piece to our game that is missing: our ball!

■ **Note**   For more information on setting up your system for iOS development, please refer to the Unity documentation on iPhone development: http://docs.unity3d.com/Manual/ iphone-GettingStarted.html.

Add the Ball

Finally we will add the main object of our game. The ball is what will be used by the player of our game to remove the bricks, obtain power-ups, and simply amaze with cool effects. Initially the game will start with one ball located on the paddle in the middle of the screen. During gameplay we will have additional balls introduced from certain bricks in order to make things both more challenging and fun for our players.

1. To add the ball, navigate to the Assets/Sprites folder in the Project View.

2. Select the object named ball and drag it to the Hierarchy View. This will add the ball at the lower left of our background in the Scene View.

3. Next change the Transform properties of Position X to 8 and Y to 1.3.

4. Also change the Scale for both X and Y to 3. Our Scene View should now look like Figure 2-19.

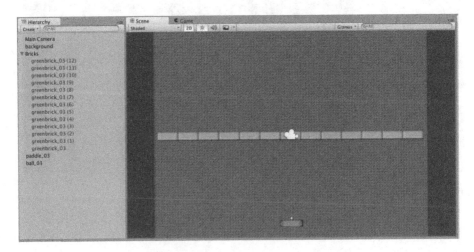

Figure 2-19. Ball over our Paddle in our game

We now have the bare minimum setup for our classic bricks game. While there is no movement or interactivity yet we can see how the game is coming together. We finalize what we are doing in this chapter by saving our Scene.

Summary

In this chapter we discussed the basics of a 2D game project setup in Unity. We walked through the basic framework and layout of the key components of a Brick Breaker game including bricks, paddle, and ball.

In the next chapter we will start to add interactivity to each of our game assets and begin the establishment of game play.

Don't panic.

—Douglas Adams, *Hitchhiker's Guide to the Galaxy*

CHAPTER 3

■ ■ ■

Create Positioning and Movement

One of the most important parts of our game is the level of interactivity and movement centered around effective game play. How we position the objects on the screen and the way we create interactive movement will help our game player understand and enjoy our game play.

In Chapter 2 we learned about the various layout options that Unity provides for developers to tailor their environment preferences. In this chapter we will add movement to our paddle and ball. In addition we will learn about how to script the objects involved in our game.

Let's get the ball rolling!

Making Our Ball Move

In the last chapter we ended our initial game layout process by adding a ball to our scene. The ball sits right about our paddle and acts the main character of interactivity for our brick breaking game. However right now our ball is pretty small and doesn't do anything when we play our game. Let's make our ball a little bigger in the scene by increasing the size relative to our paddle.

Click on the Sprites folder and select the ball sprite we imported. In the Inspector view on the right you will see the properties of the Sprite. Modify the Pixel per Unit size by changing the number 100 to 50 (Figure 3-1).

Figure 3-1. *Ball Sprite settings in the Inspector*

Changing the option in the Inspector will resize our ball based on the world units defined in Unity. One world unit equates to 1 meter so setting the object to 50 means 50 meters in the game space. Figure 3-2 displays the new larger ball sitting on the paddle in our scene.

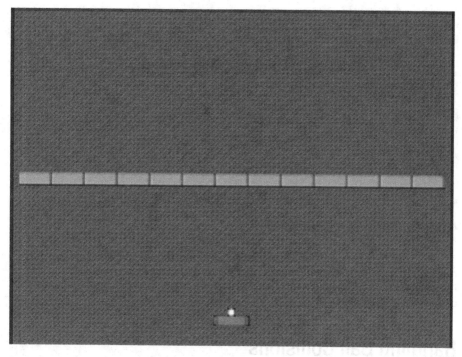

Figure 3-2. Resized ball on the paddle object in our scene

■ **Note** The Pixels per Unit can also be adjusted without typing by using the mouse. Hover your cursor over the text in the Inspector to see the Unity drag and scale feature. Hold the left mouse key and drag left or right to increase or decrease the scale.

The larger-sized ball makes it easier to see and collide with our brick objects. It also looks more prominent in our scene. Next we will make our ball move in the scene.

In order to see the movement in the ball, let's elevate the object over the paddle some. Select the ball object in the Hierarchy View. In the Inspector change the Transform Y property from 1.3 to 2.0. This will place the ball over the paddle at a higher point in the scene so we can watch it drop.

Now with the ball still selected, click the Add Component option in the Inspector. Select Physics 2D from the list and then select Rigidbody 2D. This will add a Rigidbody to our ball that contains the options for physics aspects for movement. Figure 3-3 shows the options available to us. For now we will leave the defaults and test our ball by pressing the Play button of our game. Our ball should now fall through the bottom of our scene and off the screen.

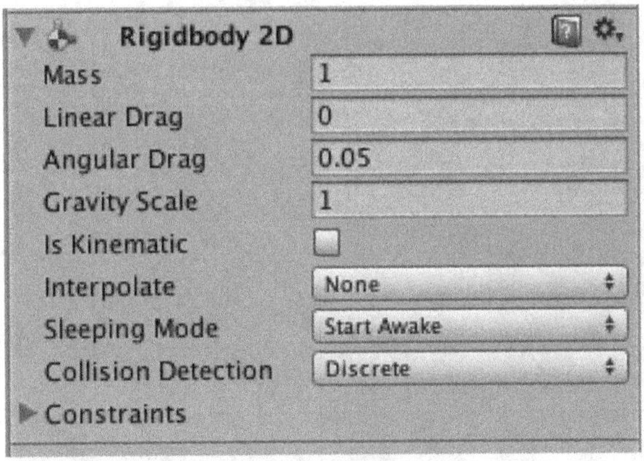

Figure 3-3. *Rigidbody options for our ball object*

With the physics engine for 2D, objects can only move in the XY plane and can only rotate on an axis that is perpendicular to that plane. We have a lot of control within the Inspector for customizing our ball, but the real power comes from dynamic changes we can add through scripting.

Handling Ball Collisions

With the Rigidbody on our ball we now have gravity and motion on our ball. However right now the object falls through whatever else is in the scene. The object does not detect any other objects in the scene (like our paddle) even though they are visible to us. The reason this occurs is that we need to add the collision detection to the objects that we want to interact with in our game. Unity provides an easy way for us to do that with a component called Colliders.

Colliders are often invisible and define the shape of an object for the purposes of physical collisions. For our ball object to detect the objects around it, we will need to add a collider to it and the objects we want to be detected. Add a collider to our ball by selecting the object in the Hierarchy View, navigating to the Inspector View on the right and clicking add component. Select Physics 2D and then the Circle Collider. If you zoom in closer to our object in the scene you will see a green circle around the white of our ball as in Figure 3-4.

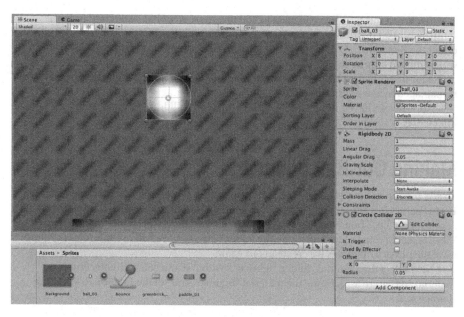

Figure 3-4. *Circle Collider around the ball object*

If we press Play in our scene our ball will still fall through the paddle. That is because our paddle needs to have its own collider added to it as well. Click on the paddle in the Hierarchy View and view to the Inspector on the right. Select add component and select Box Collider from the list. This will add a green square around our paddle to show that we have a collider around it. Now press Play in the scene and our ball will land on the paddle.

■ **Note**   You can find out more information on the different types of 2D colliders in the Unity Manual here: http://docs.unity3d.com/Manual/CollidersOverview.html. The collision action matrix is very useful for understanding the impacts of the different colliders on objects.

With our ball successfully landing on our paddle we may think that we have completed our paddle setup. Unfortunately this assumption would not be correct. The collider we just added to our paddle is static and will not work correctly in our game. To complete our setup we will need to add a Rigidbody to our paddle like we did with the ball object.

Select the paddle in the Hierarchy View again and click Add Component in the Inspector. Select Physics 2D and then Rigidbody 2D to add the Rigidbody to our paddle. If we click Play in our scene, we will now see the ball and the paddle fall off the Game View. This is, of course, not what we want to happen.

To correct this issue we will need to add one more step that is different from the setup of our ball Rigidbody. In the Inspector for the paddle, click the box "Is Kinematic" under the Rigidbody 2D component. Selecting this option informs Unity that the object will be moved only by its Transform and not by the physics engine. This feature is very useful for things like a platform or our paddle since we don't want their mass or gravity to be managed by the physics engine.

Now that we have our ball and paddle setup with colliders, let's make our ball more interactive.

Making Our Ball Bounce

To add friction or bounce to an object, Unity provides something called Physics Material. For 2D games it is actually called Physics Material 2D and can be created through the Assets menu. Let's build ours by first Right-clicking on the Assets folder in the Project View. Select Create Folder and name the folder Materials. We will use this folder to store all of the physics materials we create in our game.

Next select the Materials folder, right-click within it and select Create/Physics Material 2d (Figure 3-5). Name the material "bounce" and set the Friction to 0 and the Bounce to 1.

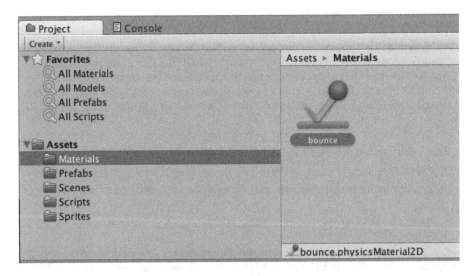

Figure 3-5. Physics material with appropiate name

The physics material needs to be added to the collider of our ball game object for it to work. Select the ball in the Hierarchy View and drag/drop the bounce material to the Circle Collider in the Inspector View (Figure 3-6).

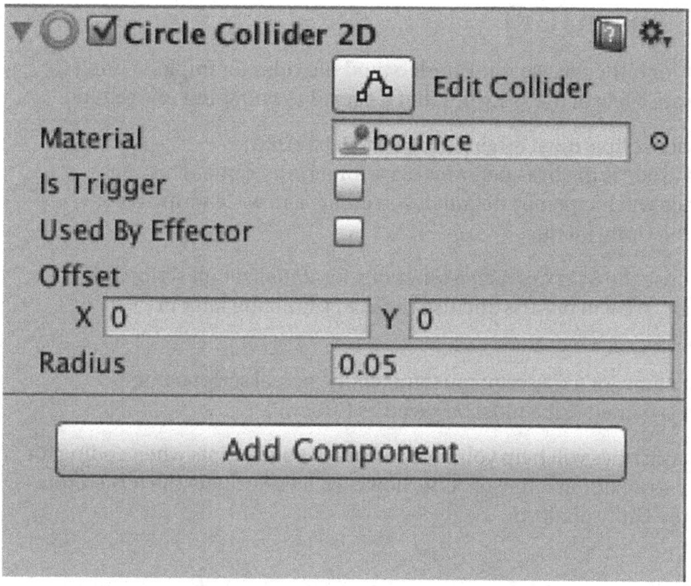

Figure 3-6. *Bounce material added to our ball*

Press Play for the scene and you should see the ball bouncing on our paddle. Right now the ball only bounces up and down to the same height in the scene, but we will correct this later.

Beginning Scripting

So far we have used the Unity editor to create all of our objects and our movement. However, in order to create the movement of our paddle using our mouse, we will need to write our first Unity script. Unity offers three scripting language options for developers to choose from. Developers can use the JavaScript, C#, or Boo language to write custom code for their games. It's a good idea to start with a language that you are familiar with or that is close in syntax to a language you typically code in.

For the purposes of this book we will be writing all scripts in C#. C# provides more flexibility but involves a steeper learning curve for coders with limited experience. C# is a true object-oriented language so it could require that beginners learn and understand advanced coding logic for certain implementations. In addition with C#, you do have full access to the .NET library and therefore potentially additional flexibility.

The Rules of C Sharp (C#)

Since we are using C# for our code, we must understand the rules for implementing C# scripts in Unity. Here are a few of the key rules that we need to know and understand:

- All behavior scripts must inherit from MonoBehaviour. MonoBehaviour is the base behavior class for a Unity game. This inheritance will happen by default if you create a new C# script through the Unity menu.

- You must use the Start or Awake functions for initialization script commands. We will discuss and use the Start function later in this chapter.

- The class name for a C# script must match the actual script name (i.e., a class named Cube must be saved as Cube.cs).

Knowing these basic rules will help you avoid errors in your scripts when coding for C#. Before we actually write our first line of code, however, let's evaluate the text editors available to use with the Unity platform.

Selecting an Editor

In order to write a script in Unity, you will need use a text editor. By default, Unity comes with its own propriety editor called MonoDevelop. However, let's look a few text editors that Unity supports for developers:

- Notepad++ (Windows) - It is a free text editor designed to replace the basic Notepad application installed by default on Windows. The application supports numerous programming languages and offers various features to make editing text easier.

- TextWrangler (Mac) - Similar to BBEdit, TextWrangler is a feature-rich; free, plain text editor. It is considered to be a powerful tool for transforming and modifying plain text.

- MonoDevelop - A cross platform integrated development environment (IDE) editor created for writing code in many programming languages. This is the default editor for Unity.

MonoDevelop is the editor that will be referenced for the examples in this book.

Our First Script

Let's go ahead and create our first script. First navigate to the Project View and select the drop-down menu at the top, next to the word Create.

As I mentioned in the beginning of this chapter, we will code in C# for a majority of our scripts. Therefore, click on C# Script on the menu. This will create a new script for us in the Asset folder with a default name of "NewBehaviourScript." The name will be highlighted so we can edit it to our own unique name. Go ahead and change the name to Paddle. We will be adding this script to the paddle we created earlier.

■ **Note** If you do not set a name for your script, you could see the error "The namespace 'global::' already contains a definition for 'NewBehaviourScript'." This error means you left another script named the default name in your project. It will go away if you rename NewBehaviourScript to something else.

For cleanliness, let's drag the new script we created into the Scripts folder under Assets in the Project View. Now double-click on the Paddle script in your Project View. This will open the script in the editor that you configured, which by default should be MonoDevelop.

When the script first opens, it will have the default constructor set up for us. Listing 3-1 shows us what this will look like.

Listing 3-1. Basic default layout of a C# script

```
using UnityEngine;
using System.Collections;

public class Paddle : MonoBehaviour {

    // Use this for initialization
    void Start () {

    }

    // Update is called once per frame
    void Update () {

    }
}
```

Let's break down this basic script created for us. The Start() method is called once in the lifetime of an object and first before the Update() method is called. It is only called if the instance of the script is enabled.

The Update() method runs multiple times a second since it is right before creating a frame in the Scene. Most of the game behavior (besides physics code) is typically scripted in the Update() method. Figure 3-7 shows how the script looks once we open it in the MonoDevelop editor.

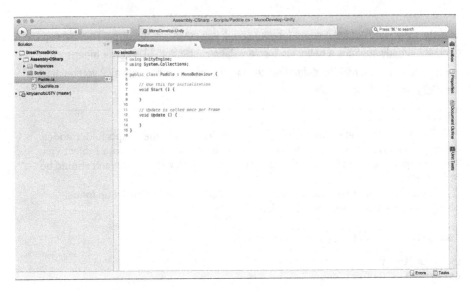

Figure 3-7. *MonoDevelop view of the Paddle script*

Now that we have a basic understanding of the initial methods, let's add some code in them. Let's change our code to match Listing 3-2.

Listing 3-2. Adding a variable and the print statements

```
using UnityEngine;
using System.Collections;

public class Paddle : MonoBehaviour {
        public int i=0;

        // Use this for initialization
        void Start () {
                print("This is my first Unity script!");
        }

        // Update is called once per frame
        void Update () {
                print(Input.mousePosition);
        }
}
```

So what did we just do? Well we first defined a public variable named I and set the value to 0. Then, we added a print statement with a message in our Start() method. This will output the text "This is my first Unity script!" in the Unity console located next to the Project View in our scene (see Figure 3-8). Next we added the mouse position details to the Update section so the information on the location of our mouse will print out whenever we move it. OK, let's run it. Click the Save button in MonoDevelop (or press command S on a Mac) to save our Paddle.cs script.

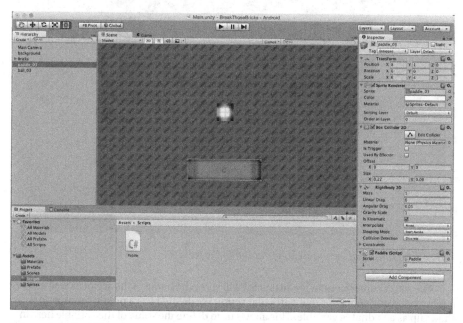

Figure 3-8. *Paddle.cs script added to the Paddle object*

■ **Note** If the script does not show in the Inspector with the correct updated information, verify that you saved the information in MonoDevelop and refresh the script. Refreshing is done by right-clicking on the script and selecting Refresh from the menu.

Our script is now created and saved. However it is not tied to any of the objects in our scene so it will not run. Let's add the Paddle.cs script to our paddle object for it to execute. Select the Hierarchy View and choose the paddle object. Next navigate to the Scripts folder in the Project View and select the Paddle.cs script. Drag and drop the script in the Inspector of the paddle object to add the script to it. You should now see the script attached to the object (Figure 3-9).

51

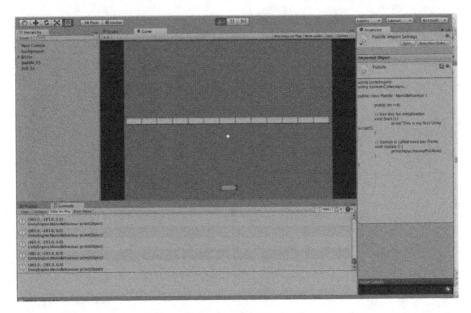

Figure 3-9. Output of the mouse information in the console

The script component in the Inspector will show the name of the script as well as the public variables defined for that particular script. We defined I as a public variable so it shows up as an editable variable. This allows us to define the value of the variable here in the Inspector before the game runs or even change it dynamically as the game is running.

Press Play on the Scene and click on the Console View. We should see the statement that we created and constantly updating information on the position of our mouse (Figure 3-9). We will use this information in the next section as we move our paddle across the screen.

Moving the Paddle with the Mouse

Our paddle has a script attached to it that we can modify to achieve movement. We want the paddle to attach to our mouse pointer on the X axis only so that it moves from left to right across our screen. Let's start by modifying our script to match Listing 3-3.

Listing 3-3. Updated script to make the paddle move

```
using UnityEngine;
using System.Collections;

public class Paddle : MonoBehaviour {

    public int i=0;
```

```
// Use this for initialization
void Start () {
    print("This is my first Unity script!");
}

// Update is called once per frame
void Update () {

    //Set variable for current position
    Vector3 paddlePos = new Vector3 (8f, this.transform.position.y, 0f);

    //Get mouse position
    float mousePos = Input.mousePosition.x / Screen.width * 16;

    //Set new mouse X position
    paddlePos.x = Mathf.Clamp(mousePos, 0.5f, 15.5f);

    //Change paddle to match new X position
    this.transform.position = paddlePos;
}

}
```

In our updated script we have now modified the Update() method to connect our paddle to the position of the mouse on the X axis. Let's walk through the script line by line so we understand how everything works together.

```
//Set variable for current position
Vector3 paddlePos = new Vector3 (8f, this.transform.position.y, 0f);
```

In this line we define the current Paddle position as a Vector3 variable. The variable allows us to set the X, Y, and Z coordinates for our current object (in this case, the paddle) dynamically. We already have the information on our paddle defined based on the logical world unit based spacing of our game scene. The only changes we will make will be to the X position in our object's Transform so we can keep the existing y information. The Z axis is not relevant for us since we are building a 2D game. Therefore we can simply define it as 0f. The f after our number stands for float since the Vector requires the use of float values.

```
//Get mouse position
float mousePos = Input.mousePosition.x / Screen.width * 16;
```

The next line grabs the current mouse X position in the Scene and sets it as a float variable. There are numerous input types and the mouse position is one of them. We also divide it by the screen width multiplied by 16 to keep the paddle centered on the mouse pointer. The 16 value represents the number of world units for our screen (refer to Chapter 1). This will allow us to see our paddle clearly and move it across the screen smoothly.

```
//Set new mouse X position
paddlePos.x = Mathf.Clamp(mousePos, 0.5f, 15.5f);
```

This line in the code sets the paddle position to the variable that we defined for the floating mouse position. It also uses a method defined as `Mathf.Clamp()` to restrict the paddle to the width of the screen. Without this restriction, the paddle would be able to leave the screen on the left or the right when the player pulls the mouse off the screen. We set the restriction to 0.5f on the left and 15.5f on the right since our screen is 16 world units long. This will allow enough of the paddle to leave the screen without going completely out of view from the player.

```
//Change paddle to match new X position
this.transform.position = paddlePos;
```

Finally we add the code to change the actual position of the paddle to the new position that we have created using variables. The `this` identifier lets Unity know that we are referencing the object that the script is connected to. The line modifies the transform of that object to the new position of where the mouse is located.

OK, we are done with our paddle script for now. Let's test it out by saving our script in MonoDevelop and playing our scene. You should now be able to move the paddle back and forth across the scene but now outside of the game. Cool beans!

Launching the Ball with the Mouse

We have our paddle setup with our ball falling on it. When you look at the older paddle games like Arkanoid and Super Breakout, the ball usually starts connected to the paddle. Let's connect our ball to the paddle and have it launch on start by adding a script to our ball.

First let's follow the steps we did before to create our Paddle script. Navigate to the Scripts folder under Assets in the Project View. Right-click on the folder and select create C# script. Name the script Ball and double-click on the file. Modify the script to match the syntax of Listing 3-4.

Listing 3-4. Ball script

```
using UnityEngine;
using System.Collections;

public class Ball : MonoBehaviour {

    public Paddle paddle;
    private bool gameStarted = false;
    private Vector3 paddleVector;

    // Use this for initialization
    void Start () {
        //Set the ball on the paddle position
        paddleVector = this.transform.position - paddle.transform.position;
    }
```

```
// Update is called once per frame
void Update () {
    if(!gameStarted){
        this.transform.position = paddle.transform.position +
        paddleVector;
            if(Input.GetMouseButtonDown(0)){
                print("Mouse clicked!");
                gameStarted = true;
                this.GetComponent<Rigidbody2D>().velocity = new Vector2
                (2f,10f);
            }
        }
    }
}
```

■ **Note** In order for the scripts to execute in the correct order, you can set it under Edit, Project Settings, Script Execution Order. If you run into any challenges with the script objects not being identified it may make sense to set the order manually.

Save the script in MonoDevelop and refresh the script in the Scripts folder. Next drag and drop the script onto our ball object in the object Inspector similar to what we did for our paddle. For our ball to sit on our paddle we need to also change the Y position of the ball object to 1.3. Our scene should now look like Figure 3-10.

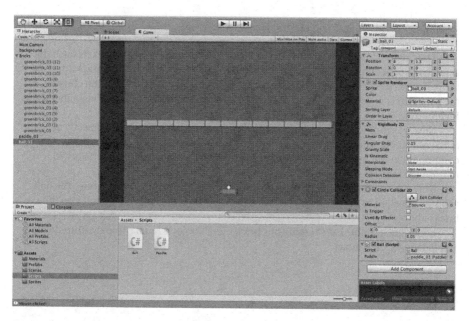

Figure 3-10. Paddle with ball attached

55

Now let's walk through the script so we understand the key components.

```
public Paddle paddle;
private bool gameStarted = false;
private Vector3 paddleVector;
```

We start by defining the variables we will use in the script. The Paddle object is our paddle defined in the scene. We make the variable public so we can access it from the Inspector. The next two private variables represent the true/false value for whether our game has started and the ball position relative to the paddle.

```
//Set the ball on the paddle position
        paddleVector = this.transform.position - paddle.transform.position;
```

Next in our Start() method we populate our paddleVector variable with the difference between the ball transform position and the paddle position. This will place the ball right on top of the paddle when the scene starts. Now let's check the update to decide when to launch the ball.

```
if(!gameStarted){
    this.transform.position = paddle.transform.position + paddleVector;
        if(Input.GetMouseButtonDown(0)){
            print("Mouse clicked!");
            gameStarted = true;
            this.GetComponent<Rigidbody2D>().velocity = new Vector2
            (2f,10f);
        }
    }
```

The final section of our code is in the Update() method. We will check to see if the game has not been started. If it has not started we will make sure the ball stays attached to the paddle as it is moved. If the mouse is clicked we display a message in the console, set the gameStarted Boolean to true, and launch the ball object to a specific velocity for the Rigidbody.

Next let's modify our Ball object slightly to ensure that it launches correctly in our Scene. In the Hierarchy View select the Ball object and look at the Rigidbody 2D component in the Inspector View. Change the Gravity Scale attribute to 0. This will remove the force of gravity on our Ball object.

Now you can test the Scene by pressing Play. When you move your mouse the ball will stay attached to the paddle object. If you click screen the ball will launch into the bricks above.

Looks great, right? Let's modify our brick prefab objects to take impact from the ball and disappear on contact.

Destroy the Blocks on Hit

In this section we will modify our bricks to accept collision by the ball and to disappear once hit. Right now when our ball touches a brick it floats right through it. This is because our ball has a collider and Rigidbody attached to it but our brick does not. Let's update our brick prefab object to allow for and react to ball collisions.

First in the Project View, navigate to the PreFab folder under Assets. Highlight the green brick object to view the Inspector on the right-hand side. Next add the Rigidbody2D and Box Collider components by following the steps we did for adding colliders to our platform. Don't forget to select the Is Kinematic check box on the Rigidbody 2D component as well. Next change the Sleeping Mode selection in the drop-down to "Start Asleep" so our bricks do not interact with anything until impacted by the Ball object. When completed your green brick object should look like Figure 3-11.

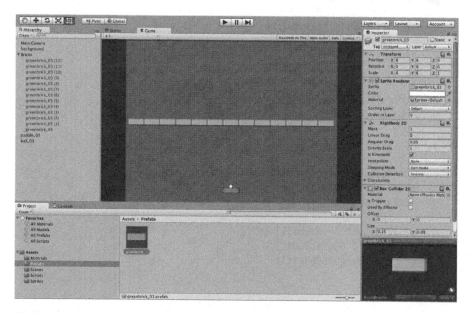

***Figure 3-11.** Brick with Rigidbody and Box Collider attached*

■ **Note** Typically for a brick in this type of game we would only need to use a box collider since it doesn't move. However, we may want to move our brick in the future to add a different type of game play so the Rigidbody is necessary.

Now press Play on your Scene and launch your ball. You should see your ball bounce off the brick when it hits it and return back to the paddle.

The last step is to add a script to our brick to destroy it when it is touched. Select the Script folder under Assets in the Project View. Right-click on the folder and select Create, C# Script. Name the script "Brick" and double-click on it. Now modify the Brick script to match Listing 3-5.

Listing 3-5. Brick script with Destroy

```
using UnityEngine;
using System.Collections;

public class Brick : MonoBehaviour {

    public int maxHits;
    public int timesHit;

    // Use this for initialization
    void Start () {
        timesHit = 0;
    }

    // Update is called once per frame
    void Update () {

    }

    void OnCollisionEnter2D(Collision2D col){
        print ("Ouch you hit me!");
        timesHit++;

        if (timesHit == maxHits) {
            print ("Destroyed!");
            Destroy(gameObject);
        }
    }

}
```

Again, let's walk through our script so we understand what is going on.

```
    public int maxHits;
    public int timesHit;

    // Use this for initialization
    void Start () {
        timesHit = 0;
    }
```

The first thing we do is set the variables that will keep track of the max number of times each brick can be hit and the number of times each brick is hit. This will allow us to enhance our game play by allowing for different brick types within our game that react to single or multiple hits by the ball. In the Start() method we simple set the default value of timesHit to 0 to start the game.

```
void OnCollisionEnter2D(Collision2D col){
        print ("Ouch you hit me!");
        timesHit++;

        if (timesHit == maxHits) {
            print ("Destroyed!");
            Destroy(gameObject);
        }
}
```

Finally we override the OnCollisionEnter2D() method for our brick Box Collider to track when the object is touched. Method overriding is an object-oriented programming feature that allows us to rewrite a specific implementation of a method provided by a parent class. We print out a message when the object is hit and increase the variable timesHit by 1. Then we check to see if the number of times hit matches the maximum times allowed for our brick object. If it matches then we destroy our game object with is the current object that the script is connected to.

■ **Note**   Read more about the OnCollisionEnter2D enter method in the documentation here: http://docs.unity3d.com/ScriptReference/MonoBehaviour. OnCollisionEnter2D.html.

Once our script is updated in MonoDevelop, select File and Save to complete the update. Then return to the Unity editor to refresh the script. Drag the Brick script to the PreFab green brick object in the Inspector. This will add the script to all of our bricks since we are modifying the PreFab object (Figure 3-12). Modify the Max Hits to 1 and leave the Times Hit option at 0.

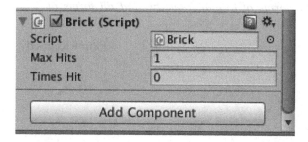

Figure 3-12. Brick script added to the green brick PreFab object

Press Play to start the game and launch the ball in the game view. When the ball strikes the brick it will disappear from the scene (Figure 3-13).

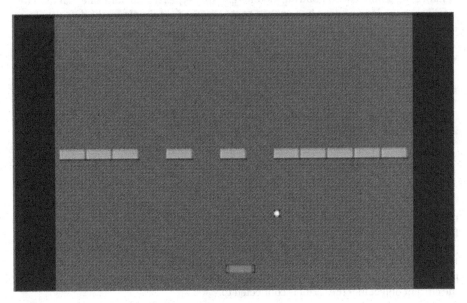

Figure 3-13. *Bricks being destroyed when the ball hits them*

Summary

In this chapter we created movement for the key objects in our game. We created our first scripts and learned what each section of the scripts meant. In addition we learned how to launch a ball with the mouse click and destroy the bricks in our scene.

In the next chapter we will continue adding interactive functionality to our game. We will learn how to keep the ball within the scene and add some sound effects to our objects.

The world is very different now. For man holds in his mortal hands the power to abolish all forms of human poverty, and all forms of human life.

—John F Kennedy

■ ■ ■

CHAPTER 4

Scripting a Game Manager

In the last chapter we built the basic structure of the game. We have our bricks, paddle, and ball together in the scene and can destroy bricks by launching our ball. The game still needs the logic to keep track of how many bricks were destroyed and the framing of our scene to keep our ball in play.

In this chapter we will work with colliders to frame our scene and limit the area our ball can travel. We will also build a Game Manager object and script to control some of the objects in the game. In addition we add display text so our user knows the current game state.

Let's make it happen!

Keeping Our Ball in the Game Space

When we play our game now, the ball will bounce and destroy the bricks in our scene. However, when the ball gets to the edges of our scene, it will travel right off the screen and leave us in an unplayable game state. (Figure 4-1) You can see how our game players would not be happy if the ball disappears off the screen to never return.

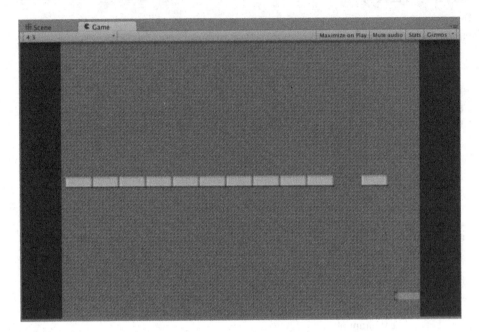

Figure 4-1. *No ball on the scene*

We will begin this chapter by adding colliders to the borders of our game play area. The colliders on the top, left, and right will act as bumpers to keep our ball in the main play area for our user. The bottom collider will act as a notifier to let us know that the user missed the ball and to end the level.

Creating Invisible Collider Walls

In Chapter 3 we were introduced to the use of colliders and how our ball responds to collisions in the game play space. In order for our ball to stay in the scene, we will create invisible colliders surrounding our game space for the ball to react to.

First let's create an empty game object in our scene. Using the top menu in the Unity editor, select GameObject and then Create Empty. Rename the object to "Game Area" by modifying the name in the Inspector. We will use this object to keep all of our play space pieces. Let's drag the object to the top of the Hierarchy view under the Main Camera object. In the Inspector of the Play Area object, select the gear at the top right of the Transform component. This will give you the option to reset the game object in the scene. Click reset to move the object to the bottom left of our scene.

Next drag the background object under the Play Area object so that it is associated with the play area. This will tidy up our design area and make it easier to identify the play area pieces. Once you have completed all of the steps your Hierarchy View should look like Figure 4-2.

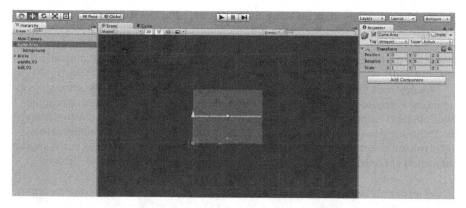

Figure 4-2. Cleaned-up Hierarchy view with new Play Area game object

---

■ **Note**   Be sure to press enter after changing the name in the Inspector. Otherwise the name of your GameObject may not retain the change

---

Now let's add another empty game object to our scene by following the same steps. Name this game object "Left Side" and reset the position to the origin in the Transform as well. Move the new object under the Play Area in the Hierarchy Window. This game object will act as the left wall of our game play area.

Under the Inspector View, select Add Component, choose Physics 2D and then Box Collider 2D. You should now have a small invisible box area on your screen in the origin position of the game. This is the collider that will repel the ball back into our play area so we will need to resize it to the game height. To position the wall correctly we will need to modify our Box Collider 2D attributes to match Figure 4-3.

```
▼ ☐ ☑ Box Collider 2D                    ☐ ✿,
                    [ ⚐ ]  Edit Collider
    Material           None (Physics Materiɑ  ⊙
    Is Trigger         ☐
    Used By Effector   ☐
    Offset
        X  -0.5              Y  6
    Size
        X  1                Y  12
```

Figure 4-3. Box Collider attributes for the Left Side game object

Next let's create the right buffer by duplicating the Left Side. This can be accomplished by right-clicking on the Left Side game object in the Hierarchy View and selecting duplicate. Rename the created Object to "Right Side," change the X under the Transform section from 0 to 16 and the Offset X under the Box Collider 2D component from -0.5 to 0.5.

We now have both a left and right side for our play area. Next follow the same steps to create the top collider for the game area. Duplicate the Right Side object and change the Box Collider 2D component to have an Offset X=0 Y=0.5 and Size X=18 Y=1. Also change the Transform positions of X to 8 and Y to 12. This will place an invisible collider at the top of the game area. Figure 4-4 shows how our play area looks now. As you see the area is completely enclosed by our colliders so there is no way for our ball to escape the area.

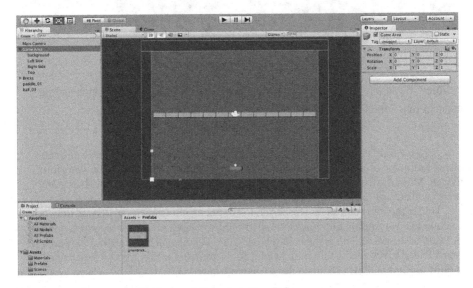

Figure 4-4. Our scene with the top, left, and right colliders

> ■ **Note** You may have noticed that the coordinates we define for our play area are based on the 16 world units spacing that we defined in Chapter 1.

OK, now save your scene (File, Save Scene) and the game by pressing Play in the Game View. Even if your ball bounces on the sides of the scene, it will not leave the play area.

Changing the Impact of Gravity

If you tried playing the game when testing the walls in the last section, you may have noticed that our ball does not have much force. The ball launches up to our bricks but does not have enough power to reach to the top of our game. We can modify the gravity of the ball to make it work better in our game but we don't want to do this. We want all of the objects in our game to start with the same gravity impact and only modify directly when we are adding feature functionality.

The best approach for improving the motion of our ball is to change the gravity definition in the game. You can accomplish this by modifying the 2D Physics Settings of the game. In the Unity Editor top menu, select Edit, Project Settings, and Physics 2D. This will open the Physics 2D Settings in the Inspector View and allow us to change the gravity defined for the project.

The default gravity is defined as X=0 Y=-9.81 as displayed in Figure 4-5. Let's change the Y attribute to -1 and then test our game. Now when we run our game our ball will bounce all the way to the top of the screen in the Game View. We can play the game to eliminate all the bricks in the scene, and the ball will keep bouncing within our play area with velocity since the impact of the gravity has been reduced.

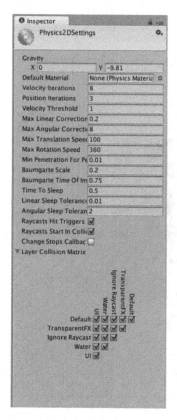

Figure 4-5. Physics 2D Settings that include gravity for the project

OK, things are looking really good in our scene. Now let's clean up the project some so we can standardize the objects in our scene.

Relabeling the Game Objects in Our Scene

In order to begin some of the advanced scripting in our game, we need to tidy up our project a bit. Some of our game objects have weird names that were created when we duplicated or added them to our scene. In this section we will relabel these objects so they will be easier to find and identify when writing our scripts. Table 4-1 describes each of the objects that need to be modified.

Table 4-1. Summary of the Objects to be Modified

GameObject	Relabeling
Ball_03	Ball
Paddle_03	Paddle
greenbrick_03 (x)	Brick

Now that you have modified your objects your Hierarchy View should look like Figure 4-6. With the main pieces of our game uniformly named, we can build the object that will manage the flow of our user experience.

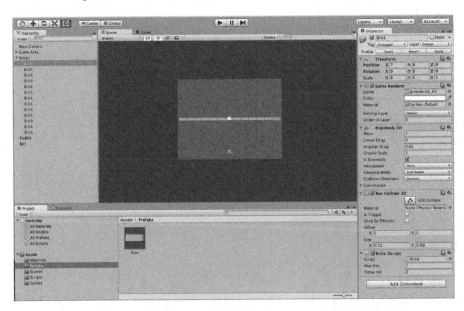

Figure 4-6. Our game objects with uniform names

■ **Note**   The green bricks can all be relabeled at once if you select them all in the Hierarchy View and change the name in the Inspector View. Another option is to accomplish this is to change the PreFab name.

Scripting Our Game Manager

In this section we will define the script that will keep track of the status of our objects. Our Game Manager script will let the game know when the user has won or lost the game, how many bricks and balls are in the scene, and instruct the game where to go based on the results of these findings. In addition the manager will start the sound aspects of our game, identifying when the game has begun and when the player has failed.

Let's begin by creating an empty GameObject to hold our script. Select GameObject, and Create Empty from the main Unity Editor menu. Rename the object to GameManager in the Inspector View and press Enter. Next click the Add Component button and select New Script. Name the script GameManager, make sure C Sharp is selected, and click the Create and Add button. Now modify the script to match Listing 4-1 below.

Listing 4-1. Game Manager Script

```
using UnityEngine;
using System.Collections;

//List of all the possible gamestates
public enum GameState
{
    NotStarted,
    Playing,
    Completed,
    Failed
}
//Require an audio source for the object
[RequireComponent(typeof(AudioSource))]

public class GameManager : MonoBehaviour {

    //Sounds to be played when entering one of the gamestates
    public AudioClip StartSound;
    public AudioClip FailedSound;

    private GameState currentState = GameState.NotStarted;

    //All the blocks found in this level, to keep track of how many are left
    private Brick[] allBricks;
    private Ball[] allBalls;
    private Paddle paddle;

    public float Timer=0.0f;
    private int minutes;
    private int seconds;
    public string formattedTime;
```

```
// Use this for initialization
 void Start () {

     Time.timeScale=1;

     //Find all the blocks in this scene
     allBricks = FindObjectsOfType(typeof(Brick)) as Brick[];

     //Find all the balls in this scene
     allBalls = FindObjectsOfType(typeof(Ball)) as Ball[];

     paddle = GameObject.FindObjectOfType<Paddle>();

     print ("Bricks:" + allBricks.Length);
     print ("Balls:" + allBalls.Length);
     print ("Paddle" + paddle);

     //Prepare the start of the level
     SwitchState(GameState.NotStarted);

 }

// Update is called once per frame
void Update () {

    switch (currentState)
    {
    case GameState.NotStarted:
        //Check if the player taps/clicks.
        if (Input.GetMouseButtonDown(0))    //Note: on mobile this will
                                            translate to the first
                                            touch/finger so perfectly
                                            multiplatform!

        {
            SwitchState(GameState.Playing);
        }
        break;

    case GameState.Playing:
    {
        Timer += Time.deltaTime;
        minutes= Mathf.FloorToInt(Timer/60F);
        seconds= Mathf.FloorToInt(Timer-minutes *60);
        formattedTime=string.Format("{0:0}:{1:00}", minutes, seconds);

        //Display Time
        //print(formattedTime);

        bool allBlocksDestroyed = false;
```

```
        //Are there no balls left?
        if (FindObjectOfType(typeof(Ball)) == null)
            SwitchState(GameState.Failed);

        if (allBlocksDestroyed)
            SwitchState(GameState.Completed);
    }
        break;
        //Both cases do the same: restart the game
    case GameState.Failed:
        print ("Gamestate Failed!");
            break;
    case GameState.Completed:
        bool allBlocksDestroyedFinal = false;

        //Destroy all the balls
        Ball[] others = FindObjectsOfType(typeof(Ball)) as Ball[];

        foreach(Ball other in others) {
            Destroy(other.gameObject);
        }
        break;
    }

}

public void SwitchState(GameState newState)
{
    currentState = newState;

    switch (currentState)
    {
    default:
    case GameState.NotStarted:
        break;

    case GameState.Playing:
        GetComponent<AudioSource>().PlayOneShot(StartSound);
        break;

    case GameState.Completed:
        GetComponent<AudioSource>().PlayOneShot(StartSound);
        break;
```

```
    case GameState.Failed:
        GetComponent<AudioSource>().PlayOneShot(FailedSound);
        break;
    }
}

}
```

Let's break down this script so we understand how it will impact our game. The first thing we do is to define the Unity libraries we are including in the script and then set an enumerated value for our game state information. An enumeration lets you create a collection of related constants that you can refer to in the game. We need to know what state the game play is in so we use an enumerator to define our state constants of Not Started, Playing, Completed, and Failed. Setting and knowing the game state will allow us to implement game state conditions that our player will experience during the game.

■ **Note** You can find out more on enumerations by viewing the video in the online Unity Manual here: https://unity3d.com/learn/tutorials/modules/beginner/scripting/enumerations.

Next we define an audio source that we will use to play our audio files. We will talk more about this later in the book.

Next we define the variables that will be accessed in the script (private) and by other objects in the game (public). These include our audio files, brick, paddle, ball, and our Timer. The timer will be used to show how long the player is playing the game.

Next we look at our Start() method that is called once when the level begins. We use a method called FindObjectsOfType() to locate all the bricks and balls in our scene and FindObjectOfType() to find our paddle. These two methods are very useful in Unity for finding objects within a Scene and is the primary reason we renamed all of our objects at the beginning of the chapter. Since all of our objects have the correct names and class scripts defined to them, we can use these methods to locate and modify the objects in our scene. We also switch the state of the game to NotStarted since the level is just beginning.

Next in our Update() method we have a Switch conditional statement that checks the state of our game and determines what will happen. Remember the Update() method is called repeatedly as the game plays so in this case it will be checking the game state repeatedly for decision making. Table 4-2 describes each case and what decisions are occurring:

Table 4-2. Summary of Cases

Case	Decision
GameState.NotStarted	If the user clicks on the mouse during this state, set the game state to Playing.
GameState.Playing	Defines and formatted the Timer. If there are no balls left in the scene, sets the game state to Failed. If there are no bricks in the scene, sets the game state to Completed.
GameState.Failed	Prints failure to console. We will use this later.
GameState.Completed	Destroys any Ball objects left in the scene since the level is done.

Finally at the bottom of our script is the method for defining sounds when our GameState changes. This script will be used later when we add sound to our game. Let's Save our script in MonoDevelop and refresh it in the Project View. Also if the script is not in your Assets, Scripts folder, please move it there now using drag and drop in the Project View. Now save your scene and press Play in the Game View. You won't see a change in the game but you should see the number of Bricks and Balls print out in the Console View (Figure 4-7).

Figure 4-7. Console View showing the number of Balls and Bricks in our Scene

Let's go ahead and add a way to know when a player has lost the ball in our game.

Scripting Our Lose Collider

Up to this point the ball in our scene was restricted to bouncing around in the game play area at the top, left, and right. If the user misses the ball with the paddle, it falls through the bottom never to be seen again. We need our game to let us know when the player has missed the ball in order for us to restart the level so that we enable them to try again. In order to accomplish this we will add an additional collider to tour the game at the bottom and call it our Lose Collider.

Begin by selecting the Top game object from the Hierarchy View. Right-click on it and select Duplicate. Rename the object to Bottom in the Inspector View and press Enter. This will give us the Bottom object in the same location as our Top game object in our Scene. Change the Y attributes in the Inspector View of the Transform to 0 and the Offset (under Box Collider 2D) to -0.5. Select the Game Area object in the Hierarchy View and your Scene View should look like Figure 4-8.

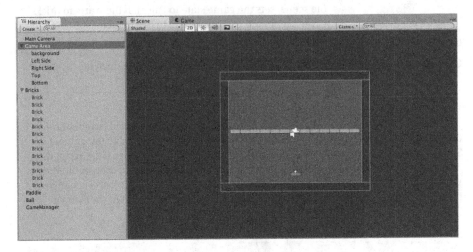

Figure 4-8. *Completely enclosed game area*

Right now our Bottom object with collider matches our other game area objects. If you press Play in the Game View and miss the ball with the paddle, the ball will stay bouncing in our scene. This is not what we want with our game so we will need to change this collider to make it work properly.

Select the Bottom object in the Hierarchy View and look at the Inspector View for our Box Collider 2D component. Click on the check box next to IsTrigger and play the game again. This time the ball will fall of the scene as it did before we added the collider. Why is that, you ask? Well when the IsTrigger option is selected on a Collider component, the Rigidbody of the colliding object is not registered. Instead the collider executes OnTrigger events that can be used to capture and define what happens when an object collides with it.

In order to define these events we will need to add a script to our Lose Collider object. In the Inspector of the Bottom object select Add Component. Select NewScript, name the script Lose, and click the Create and Add button. Our Bottom object should now look like Figure 4-9.

Figure 4-9. *Box Collider 2D in Bottom object Inspector View*

We will need to modify our script to remove the default `Start()` and `Update()` methods and include our `OnTrigger()` detection method (Listing 4-2).

Listing 4-2. Lose collider script connected to Lose object

```
using UnityEngine;
using System.Collections;

public class Lose : MonoBehaviour {
    private Ball ball;

    IEnumerator Pause() {
        print("Before Waiting 2 seconds");
        yield return new WaitForSeconds(2);

        //Find the ball and reset game start
        ball = GameObject.FindObjectOfType<Ball>();
        ball.gameStarted = false;

        //Reload level
        Application.LoadLevel(Application.loadedLevel);

        print("After Waiting 2 Seconds");
    }

    void OnTriggerEnter2D (Collider2D trigger){
        print ("Lost Triggered!");
```

```
        //Wait before restarting level
        StartCoroutine(Pause());

    }
}
```

In our new Lose script we start by declaring our Unity packages to include and a private instance of our Ball object. Then we enter the main premise of our script. We define a Coroutine that is a function executed in intervals in order to use a yield statement for returning code. This sounds complicated but really it just allows us to execute code after a certain number of seconds. This is useful for out game since it enables us to put a slight pause before resetting the level for our game player.

In the OnTriggerEnter2D() method of our script, we call the StartCoroutine() method of Unity to execute our Pause() method we define. Within the Pause() method we use the Unity yield base class instruction to tell our game to wait 2 seconds before executing the next step. The next step that will execute is to search for the ball objects in the game and to set the GameStarted Boolean of our Ball to false.

Before we can execute our game, however, we will need to modify our Ball script to make the Boolean accessible to our Lose script. Right now in the Ball script the GameStarted Boolean is private, which means only the script itself can call it. We will need to change the variable definition from private to public for this script to work. Listing 4-3 shows the updated Ball script.

Listing 4-3. Updated Ball script with public GameStarted variable

```
using UnityEngine;
using System.Collections;

public class Ball : MonoBehaviour {

    public Paddle paddle;
    public bool gameStarted = false;
    private Vector3 paddleVector;

    // Use this for initialization
    void Start () {
        //Set the ball on the paddle position
        paddleVector = this.transform.position - paddle.transform.position;
    }

    // Update is called once per frame
    void Update () {
        if(!gameStarted){
            this.transform.position = paddle.transform.position + paddleVector;
            if(Input.GetMouseButtonDown(0)){
                print("Mouse clicked!");
                gameStarted = true;
```

```
            this.GetComponent<Rigidbody2D>().velocity = new Vector2
            (2f,10f);
        }
    }
  }
}
```

■ **Note** Still don't understand Coroutines? You can find out more about them by viewing the video in the online Unity Manual here: `https://unity3d.com/learn/tutorials/modules/intermediate/scripting/coroutines`.

Now save both your Ball and you Lose Script in MonoDevelop. Right-click on the Lose or Ball script in the Project View of the Unity editor and select Refresh. Move the Lose Script to the Scripts folder under Assets. Navigate to the Game View and press Play to test the game. When you miss the ball with the paddle, the game will pause 2 seconds and reset the game.

Cool beans! Save your Scene in the Unity Editor.

Using UI Text to Display Information

Our game is working and we have defined our win/lose condition. However, our player has no idea how to start our game or whether they won or lost. We have not visually presented any instruction to the user on what to do and the result of their actions. We need to place some minimal instruction to our user and we can use the Unity UI Text object to do that.

■ **Note** Find out more about UI Text objects them by viewing the video here: `http://unity3d.com/learn/tutorials/modules/beginner/ui/ui-text`.

In Unity 4 there was an object called GUIText that was used to display text on the screen. The display was pretty generic and led to numerous third party creations to provide enhanced text. The UI Text object offers advanced text options including rich text to give the developer more control of the user interface display. The text is laid in a Canvas object that can be modified to fit the screen. Let's add a text object to our scene.

Select GameObject, UI, Text from the Unity Editor menu. This will create a UI text object in your scene and add a Canvas object to your Hierarchy View. Under the Canvas object will be a Text object containing the text "New Text." Modify the Canvas object by selecting it and navigating to the Inspector View. Change the Canvas component to match Figure 4-10.

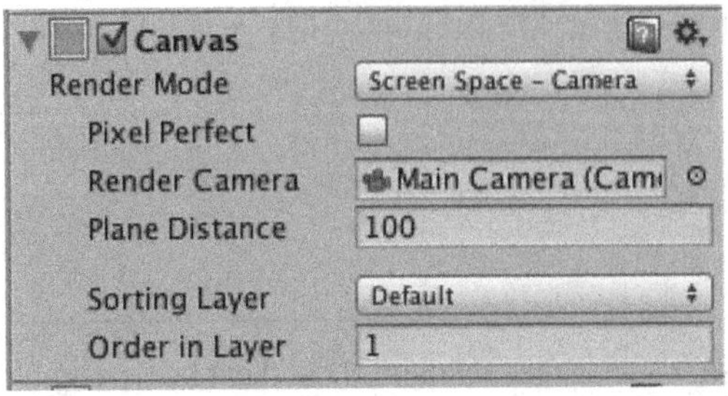

▼ ☐ ☑ **Canvas**   🖵 ✿,
  Render Mode | Screen Space – Camera ↕ |
    Pixel Perfect   ☐
    Render Camera | 🎦 Main Camera (Cam ⊙ |
    Plane Distance | 100 |
    Sorting Layer | Default ↕ |
    Order in Layer | 1 |

Figure 4-10. *Canvas object for UI Text object*

We change the Render Mode to match our screen space for our game since it is in 2D. Then click on the small icon next to the Render Camera option and select the Main Camera for our scene. This will set the size of the Canvas to the screen and place our text within the screen space. Finally, change the Order in Layer to 1 so the Canvas and Text are in the front of our scene.

Now modify the Text object by selecting it in the Hierarchy View. In the Inspector View modify the Rect Transform Pos X to 0 and Pos Y to 164. This will place the Text in the top middle of our Game View. Modify the Text (Script) component by changing the Font Size to 20 and Align to center. Figure 4-11 shows the updated Text object Inspector View, and Figure 4-12 shows how our Game View should look now.

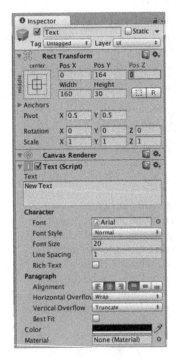

Figure 4-11. *Text component settings for the Canvas Text object*

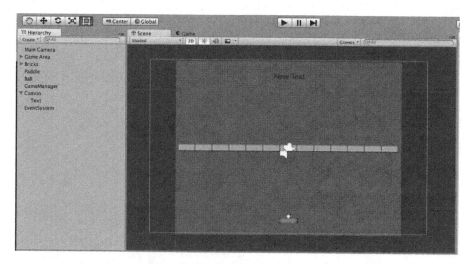

Figure 4-12. *Text object in middle of Game View*

With our text now in the middle of our screen, let's modify the Game Manager script (Listing 4-4) to find and change the text in our start and end game states.

Listing 4-4. Modified Game Manager script with Text object changing function

```
using UnityEngine;
using System.Collections;
using UnityEngine.UI;

//List of all the possible gamestates
public enum GameState
{
    NotStarted,
    Playing,
    Completed,
    Failed
}
//Require an audio source for the object
[RequireComponent(typeof(AudioSource))]

public class GameManager : MonoBehaviour {

    //Sounds to be played when entering one of the gamestates
    public AudioClip StartSound;
    public AudioClip FailedSound;

    private GameState currentState = GameState.NotStarted;
```

```
//All the blocks found in this level, to keep track of how many are left
private Brick[] allBricks;
private Ball[] allBalls;
private Paddle paddle;

public float Timer=0.0f;
private int minutes;
private int seconds;
public string formattedTime;

public Text text;

// Use this for initialization
void Start () {

    Time.timeScale=1;

    //Find all the blocks in this scene
    allBricks = FindObjectsOfType(typeof(Brick)) as Brick[];

    //Find all the balls in this scene
    allBalls = FindObjectsOfType(typeof(Ball)) as Ball[];

    paddle = GameObject.FindObjectOfType<Paddle>();

    print ("Bricks:" + allBricks.Length);
    print ("Balls:" + allBalls.Length);
    print ("Paddle" + paddle);

    //Change start text
    ChangeText ("Click To Begin");

    //Prepare the start of the level
    SwitchState(GameState.NotStarted);
}

// Update is called once per frame
void Update () {

    switch (currentState)
    {
    case GameState.NotStarted:
        //Change start text
        ChangeText ("Click To Begin");
```

```
            //Check if the player taps/clicks.
            if (Input.GetMouseButtonDown(0))    //Note: on mobile this will
                                                translate to the first
                                                touch/finger so perfectly
                                                multiplatform!
            {
                SwitchState(GameState.Playing);
            }
            break;

    case GameState.Playing:
    {
        Timer += Time.deltaTime;
        minutes= Mathf.FloorToInt(Timer/60F);
        seconds= Mathf.FloorToInt(Timer-minutes *60);
        formattedTime=string.Format("{0:0}:{1:00}", minutes, seconds);

        //Change start text
        ChangeText ("Time: "+formattedTime);

        bool allBlocksDestroyed = false;

        //Are there no balls left?
        if (FindObjectOfType(typeof(Ball)) == null)
            SwitchState(GameState.Failed);

        if (allBlocksDestroyed)
            SwitchState(GameState.Completed);
    }.
        break;
        //Both cases do the same: restart the game
    case GameState.Failed:
        print ("Gamestate Failed!");
        ChangeText ("You Lose :(");

            break;
    case GameState.Completed:
        bool allBlocksDestroyedFinal = false;

        //Destroy all the balls
        Ball[] others = FindObjectsOfType(typeof(Ball)) as Ball[];

        foreach(Ball other in others) {
            Destroy(other.gameObject);
        }
        break;
    }

}
```

```
public void ChangeText (string text) {
    //Find Canvas and modify text
    GameObject canvas = GameObject.Find("Canvas");
    Text[] textValue = canvas.GetComponentsInChildren<Text>();
    textValue[0].text = text;
}

public void SwitchState(GameState newState)
{
    currentState = newState;

    switch (currentState)
    {
    default:
    case GameState.NotStarted:
        break;

    case GameState.Playing:
        GetComponent<AudioSource>().PlayOneShot(StartSound);
        break;

    case GameState.Completed:
        GetComponent<AudioSource>().PlayOneShot(StartSound);
        break;

    case GameState.Failed:
        GetComponent<AudioSource>().PlayOneShot(FailedSound);
        break;
    }
}

}
```

In our modified script we have added a ChangeText() method that takes in a string variable. First we include our UnityEngine UI package. The string is the text displayed in our Text object replacing the "New Text" text. The method searches for the Canvas object and then finds the child Text object to place in an array. It then sets the first one it finds to the text passed into the method. Since we only have one text object in our scene, this works for our game.

■ **Note** Another option for changing the text dynamically by setting text = GetComponent<Text>(); and defining the text object using text.text = "value";

80

Let's also modify our Lose script to notify the player when they lose (Listing 4-5).

Listing 4-5. Adding of GameManager object to Lose script in order to change text when user loses

```
using UnityEngine;
using System.Collections;

public class Lose : MonoBehaviour {
    private Ball ball;
    private GameManager gameManager;

    IEnumerator Pause() {
        print("Before Waiting 2 seconds");
        //Switch GameManager State
        gameManager = GameObject.FindObjectOfType<GameManager>();
        gameManager.SwitchState (GameState.Failed);

        yield return new WaitForSeconds(2);

        //Find the ball and reset game start
        ball = GameObject.FindObjectOfType<Ball>();
        ball.gameStarted = false;

        //Reload level
        Application.LoadLevel(Application.loadedLevel);

        print("After Waiting 2 Seconds");
    }

    void OnTriggerEnter2D (Collider2D trigger){
        print ("Lost Triggered!");

        //Wait before restarting level
        StartCoroutine(Pause());

    }
}
```

In the script we have added an object for our GameManager. We then search for the GameManager in our game and switch the state to failed. We then change the text to "You Lose :(" so the player can see that they missed the ball.

Summary

In this chapter we finalize the game space of our game so the ball will not leave the play area. We build a Game Manager to control what happens in our game and to set the game states. Finally, we set up some visible text so our players could see the status of the game.

In the next chapter we will enhance our Game Manager and game play attributes. We will also begin to work with sound effects and background music for our game.

I can accept failure. Everyone fails at something. But I can't accept not trying.

—Michael Jordan

■ ■ ■

CHAPTER 5

Adding Sound and Music

Now that we have a basic Game manager in place from the last chapter, we can focus on adding audio and sound to our game. One of the key components of any game is the sounds and effects your user engages with when playing. If you think of memorable games like Angry Birds, for example, the music and sound effects made the game so much better. When the intro music of the game played, you knew someone was playing Angry Birds.

In this chapter we will add sound and sound effects to our game. We will include background music for our level and interactive sound for our game play.

Let the music begin!

Adding Background Music

Cool background music will add an element of fun and interactivity to our game. Let's add some background music to our game to add some life to our player experience. The first thing we need to do is to understand how sound works in Unity. In order to play a sound, the two components that are required are the Audio Listener and the Audio Source.

The Audio Listener acts like a microphone by receiving audio input and playing it through the device speakers. Usually there is only one listener attached in a game, and it's usually connected to the Main Camera. Figure 5-1 shows the audio listener displayed in the Inspector View that is connected to the camera in our game. There are no attributes to set for the listener since its sole purpose is to listen for audio.

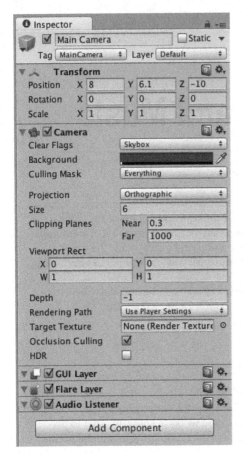

Figure 5-1. *Main Camera with Audio Listener attached*

■ **Note**   You can find out more on the Audio Listener by reviewing the Unity Manual here: http://docs.unity3d.com/Manual/class-AudioListener.html.

The Audio Source is the speaker in the Scene that plays the selected AudioClip. It works in conjunction with the Audio Listener to provide the sound experience in the game. When an Audio Source is connected to a gameobject that is in the vicinity of the Audio Listener, the sound can be heard through the speakers.

Now that we have a general idea on how this works in the game, let's add background music to our scene. Select the GameManager object in the Hierarchy View and view the Inspector View on the right. You should see a component called Audio Source already attached to the gameobject. Expand the component by clicking on the arrow so you can see the advanced options. The key option we need to modify at this point is the

"AudioClip" selection. Click the little circle to the right of the option, and this will display a selection window. Select the file Level1BGM file.

Next make sure the "Play on Awake" check box is selected. Press Play in the Game View window and you should hear background music as your game plays. Figure 5-2 shows how the Audio Source option should look in the Inspector for the GameManager.

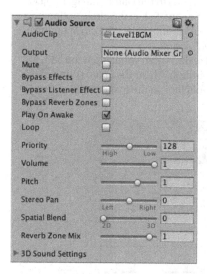

Figure 5-2. *Audio Source with options expanded*

Another key option check box to select is the "Loop" check box. This will allow our background music to replay when it ends and allow us to use a shorter looping clip. This will reduce the size of our app since our audio files can be smaller.

Adding Start and End Sounds

We have background music in the game, so let's start adding some sound effects. Initializing sound effects will guide our game player through the experience of the game. Fortunately when we built our GameManager script we already included variables for our start and end sounds in the script. The beginning of our script includes the following details:

```
//Require an audio source for the object
[RequireComponent(typeof(AudioSource))]

public class GameManager : MonoBehaviour {

    //Sounds to be played when entering one of the gamestates
    public AudioClip StartSound;
    public AudioClip FailedSound;
```

The `RequireComponent()` function specifies what components need to be included for the script to function correctly. It will add the required component automatically to the game object that helps prevent scripting errors. We set the `AudioSource` as required since we are adding sounds to this object. Next we set the variables for the `AudioClip` objects for our start and fail sounds in the game.

To add the start and end sounds to the script, navigate to the GameManager object Inspector and expand the GameManager script component. Select the circle option next to the Start Sound option and select the "game-started" sound. Select the circle option next to the Failed Sound and select the "game-ended" sound.

Play the game now and you should hear a start sound when you launch the ball. If you miss the ball by letting it fall pass the paddle, you should hear the failed sound play. Figure 5-3 shows how the Game Manager script should look in the Inspector View now.

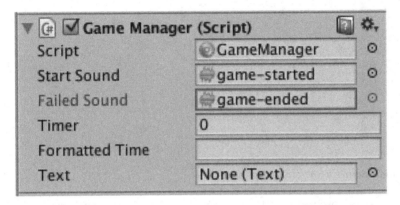

Figure 5-3. _Shows the GameManager script with sounds selected_

Let's add some sounds to our game environment now.

Bricks with Action and Impact Sound

When we play our game now, the ball bounces and removes our bricks. This is the basic structure of a brick breaker game, but without sound the play is underwhelming. To enhance the game play we should add some type of visual effect to the bricks and a sound when the ball impacts it. We will keep the effect small but the change will make our game more fun.

Let's begin by adding a simple animation to the brick. The animation will be called Woggle and will cause our brick to shrink when it is hit. Let's navigate to our `Brick` prefab object in the Assets/Prefabs folder. Select the `Brick` object, click the Add Component button, and select Animation. Under the component you will find an attribute called Animations. Change the number from 0 to 1. Now select the circle next to and select the Animation Clip called Woggle. Next unselect the "Play Automatically" check box since we want to control when the Animation is played in our script. This will add the Woggle animation effect to your brick (Figure 5-4).

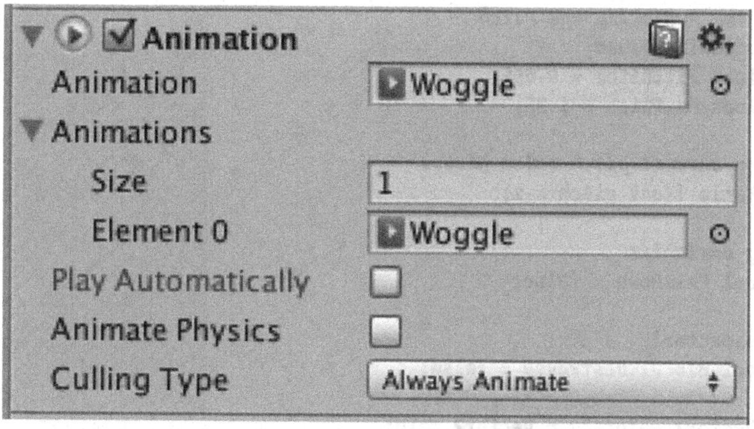

Figure 5-4. Woggle animation added to the brick Prefab object

Since we added the animation to the brick Prefab object, all of the bricks in our Scene will have the animation tied to them. Prefabs make it really easy to modify all the Bricks at once and ensure they all behave in the same way.

Modify Brick Script for Sound

Our Brick objects now have animation tied to them and that is great. However the animation will not run until we instruct it to start in the script tied to the game object. For the game play to function correctly, we only want our animation to run when the brick is impacted. Back in Chapter 3 we added a script to the Brick object to destroy it on impact (Listing 3-5). Listing 5-1 shows our modified Brick script with the changes highlighted for audio playback on impact:

Listing 5-1. Modified Brick script with additions for impact sound play

```
using UnityEngine;
using System.Collections;

//Make sure an AudioSource component on the GameObject where the script is
added.
[RequireComponent(typeof(AudioSource),typeof(Animation))]
public class Brick : MonoBehaviour {

    public int maxHits;
    public int timesHit;
    private bool BrickIsDestroyed=false;
```

```
//Define the AudioClip and Pitch
public AudioClip Sound;
public float PitchStep = 0.05F;
public float MaxPitch = 1.3F;

//Make the current pitch value global
public static float pitch = 1;

//Falling variables
public bool FallDown = false;

[HideInInspector]
public bool BlockIsDestroyed = false;

private Vector2 velocity = Vector2.zero;

// Use this for initialization
void Start () {
    timesHit = 0;
}

// Update is called once per frame
void Update () {
    if (FallDown && velocity != Vector2.zero)
    {

        Vector2 pos = (Vector2)transform.position;
        pos += velocity * Time.deltaTime;
    }
}

void OnBecameInvisible()
{
    BlockIsDestroyed = true;
    Destroy(gameObject);
}

private IEnumerator OnCollisionExit2D(Collision2D c)
{
    if (timesHit == maxHits) {
        print ("Destroyed on Exit!");

        print ("Play Woggle!");
        GetComponent<Collider2D> ().enabled = false;
```

```
        //Play the Woggle animation
        GetComponent<Animation> ().Play ();

        //Wait here for the length of the Woggle animation
        yield return new WaitForSeconds (GetComponent<Animation> ()
        ["Woggle"].length);

        //Animation Woggle has finished, now decide what to do, falldown
        or just disappear
        if (FallDown) {
            print ("Falling!");
            //Falldown to the direction the ball hit it, with a random
            speed and plus a little downwards "gravity"
            velocity = new Vector2 (0, Random.Range (1, 12.0F) * -1);
        } else {
            GetComponent<Renderer> ().enabled = false;
        }
        Destroy (gameObject);
    } else {
        print ("Max hits not reached");
    }
}

void OnCollisionEnter2D(Collision2D col){

    timesHit++;
    print ("Ouch you hit me this many times:"+timesHit);

    print ("Playing brick sound!");
    //Increase pitch
    pitch += PitchStep;

    //Limit pitch
    if (pitch > MaxPitch)
        pitch = 1;  //Reset pitch to one so it starts over with the
        lower tone

    //Apply pitch
    GetComponent<AudioSource>().pitch = pitch;

    //Play it once for this collision hit
    GetComponent<AudioSource>().PlayOneShot(Sound);

    StartCoroutine(OnCollisionExit2D(col));

}

}
```

OK, let's walk through the changes in our script and get a better understanding of what is happening. First we require our gameobject to have an Audio Source and an Animation component using the same method we did for our GameManager script.

```
//Make sure an AudioSource component on the GameObject where the script
is added.
[RequireComponent(typeof(AudioSource),typeof(Animation))]
```

Next we add the variables we need to control when the sound is played. We make the AudioClip object public so we can set it in the Inspector when placing the Brick prefab.

```
private bool BrickIsDestroyed=false;

    //Make the AudioClip and Pitch modifiable in the editor
    public AudioClip Sound;
    public float PitchStep = 0.05F;
    public float MaxPitch = 1.3F;

    //Make the current pitch value global
    public static float pitch = 1;

    //Falling variable
    public bool FallDown = false;

    [HideInInspector]
    public bool BlockIsDestroyed = false;

    private Vector2 velocity = Vector2.zero;
```

Next we include the method in our Update script for checking the FallDown variable and velocity. We check to see if the FallDown flag is enabled and then grab our Vector2 position for the gameobject. This will allow our Brick position to always be known throughout the game play.

```
if (FallDown && velocity != Vector2.zero)
{

    Vector2 pos = (Vector2)transform.position;
    pos += velocity * Time.deltaTime;
}
```

Next we have a function to play our Woggle animation and wait for the animation to complete when the collision exits. Once the animation is complete the script checks to see if the Fall Down check box is selected. If it is, then it moves the brick down in by a restricted velocity and destroy the object.

Next we need to set the variable objects in the Inspector for our Brick script. The new variable for sound is the main attribute that we need to set for now. Set the sound to the block-hit sound by selecting the circle next to the Sound attribute.

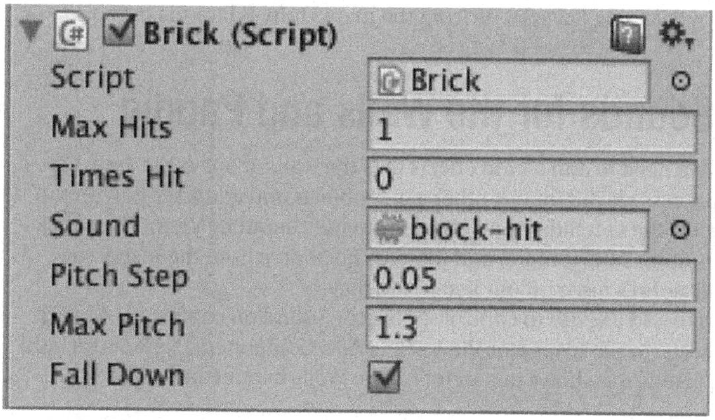

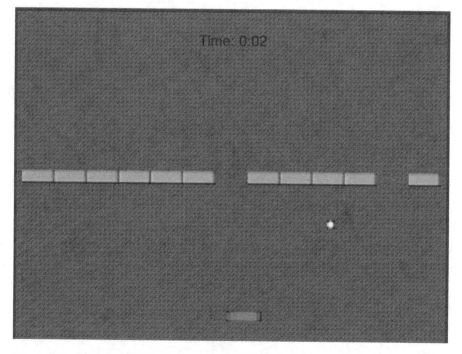

Figure 5-5. *Brick script variables set*

Finally we add an Audio Source component to our Brick object. We don't need to set the source since we have defined the block-hit sound in our Brick script to be played on hit. The sound will be placed in the Audio Source component through the script.

Press Play in the Game View and play the game. You should hear the bricks make a noise when the ball hits them and see the bricks disappear with an effect on impact (Figure 5-6).

Figure 5-6. *Minimized brick effect on contact of ball*

91

Save your scene by selecting Save Scene from the main Unity Editor file menu.

Game Area Sounds for the Walls and Paddle

One of the final areas we need to add sound effects to is the walls of our game area. We will follow the same process we did for our other game objects and add a script with the Audio Source. First select the Left Side game object from the Hierarchy View. Then click the Add Component button, Select Audio, and then Audio Source from the Inspector View. This will add the audio source for our listener to play.

Next we will need to add a script to control setting the sound on contact like we did for our other gameobjects. In the Inspector View select Add Component, New Script, and name the script Wall. Listing 5-2 shows our script for the Walls in our game area.

Listing 5-2. Walls script

```
using UnityEngine;
using System.Collections;

//Make sure there is always an AudioSource component on the GameObject where
this script is added.
[RequireComponent(typeof(AudioSource))]
public class Wall : MonoBehaviour {

    //Make the AudioClip and Pitch configurable in the editor
    public AudioClip Sound;

    // Use this for initialization
    void Start () {

    }

    // Update is called once per frame
    void Update () {

    }

    void OnCollisionEnter2D(Collision2D col){
        print ("Ouch you hit my wall!");

        //Play it once for this collision hit
        GetComponent<AudioSource>().PlayOneShot(Sound);
    }
}
```

The script is very similar to our Brick script. We start by requiring an Audio Source be attached to our gameobject and setting our public AudioClip variable. Next we define the OnCollisionEnter2D() method to print a message to the Console and set our AudioSource component to the AudioClip we defined. This will only play the sound when the wall is hit with the ball.

We then can take the steps to add the Audio Source component and Wall script to the Right Side and Top game objects in the Hierarchy View.

For our Paddle we will modify our script so that the Paddle will make a sound when the ball collides with it. Listing 5-3 shows highlights of the changes in our Paddle script.

Listing 5-3. Paddle script

```
using UnityEngine;
using System.Collections;

//Make sure there is always an AudioSource component on the GameObject where
this script is added.
[RequireComponent(typeof(AudioSource))]
public class Paddle : MonoBehaviour {

    public int i=0;
    //Make the AudioClip configurable in the editor
    public AudioClip Sound;

    // Use this for initialization
    void Start () {
        print("This is my first Unity script!");
    }

    // Update is called once per frame
    void Update () {
        //print(Input.mousePosition);
        //Set variable for current position
        Vector3 paddlePos = new Vector3 (8f, this.transform.position.y, 0f);

        //Get mouse position
        float mousePos = Input.mousePosition.x / Screen.width * 16;

        //Set new mouse X position
        paddlePos.x = Mathf.Clamp(mousePos, 0.5f, 15.5f);

        //Change paddle to match new X position
        this.transform.position = paddlePos;
    }
```

```
//OnCollisionEnter will only be called when one of the colliders has a
rigidbody
void OnCollisionEnter2D(Collision2D c)
{
    //Change the sound pitch if a slowdown powerup has been picked up
    GetComponent<AudioSource>().pitch = Time.timeScale;

    //Play it once for this collision hit
    GetComponent<AudioSource>().PlayOneShot(Sound);
}

}
```

The additions we made to the script are very similar to the Wall script with one exception. The script will modify the pitch of the sound based on the Time.timescale setting of the game. We will look more at time in the next chapter when we discuss effects of different game power-ups.

When we play our game now and allow the ball pass the bricks to the top of our scene, the ball should bounce back with a bouncy sound (Figure 5-7).

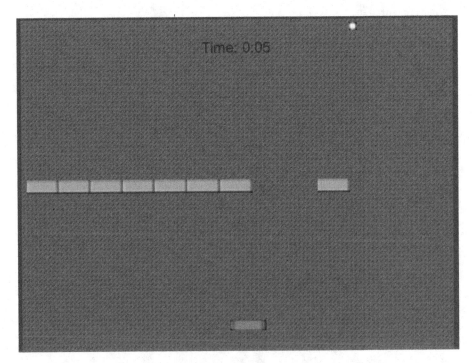

Figure 5-7. *Ball bouncing off the top of the scene and making sound*

Save your scene by selecting Save Scene from the main Unity Editor file menu.

Summary

In this chapter we added background music that plays while the player plays the game. We also added sound effects to the game objects in our game including the walls, paddle, and bricks. Finally, we set up some visible text so our players could see the status of the game.

In the next chapter we will enhance our game play by adding power-ups and particle effects to add more interactivity to the game.

> *I can accept failure. Everyone fails at something. But I can't accept not trying.*
>
> —Michael Jordan

Summary

CHAPTER 6

Game Power-Ups

When we think about the Super Breakout game, one of the key features in game play is the enhancement of the game through power-ups. Power-Ups in the game are additions or subtractions to the game play by adding a level of interactivity for the game.

In this chapter we will walk through the creation of Power-Up prefab objects for the game. We will add an extra ball and paddle resizing by allowing the game player to collect the falling prefabs.

Time to drop some power-ups!

Building Power-Up Scripts

Setting up the base class for the power-up objects will allow for us to build the foundation of our power-up prefab objects. These objects will define the key features of our game and allow certain game objects to inherit functionality. Listing 6-1 is the script for our BasePowerUp object.

Listing 6-1. Base Power-Up class

```
using UnityEngine;
using System.Collections;

[RequireComponent(typeof(Rigidbody2D), typeof(Collider2D),
typeof(AudioSource))]
public class BasePowerUp : MonoBehaviour {

    public float DropSpeed = 1; //How fast does it drop?
    public AudioClip Sound; //Sound played when the powerup is picked up

    // Use this for initialization
    void Start()
    {
        GetComponent<AudioSource>().playOnAwake = false;
    }
}
```

```
    // Update is called once per frame
    protected virtual void Update()
    {

    }

    IEnumerator OnTriggerEnter2D(Collider2D other)
    {
        //Only interact with the paddle
        if (other.name == "Paddle")
        {
            //Notify the derived powerups that its being picked up
            OnPickup();

            //Disable further collisions
            GetComponent<Collider2D>().enabled = false;
            GetComponent<Renderer>().enabled = false;

            //Change the sound pitch
            GetComponent<AudioSource>().pitch = Time.timeScale;

            //Play audio and wait
            GetComponent<AudioSource>().PlayOneShot(Sound);
            yield return new WaitForSeconds(Sound.length);
        }
    }

    //Every powerup which derives from this class should implement this.
    protected virtual void OnPickup()
    {

    }

}
```

Now let's walk through what is going on in this script. The first thing we do after requiring the Unity libraries that we need is to set the required components for the object. We want to make sure that each object that inherits from this base object has a RigidBody2D, Collider2D, and an AudioSource. The rigid body and collider allow the falling object to interact with the paddle when the two make contact. We will use this contact to trigger an event to make an effect take place in the game. The audio source will be used to play a sound when the objects collide so the user knows something has happened in the game.

After that we define our variables for how fast the object will fall in the scene and the sound that will play. Next we set our audio to not play on awake when the object starts. We only want our sound to play on impact so setting this will have the sound play only when the object is awoken.

Finally the main component of our script is the OnTriggerEnter2D() method. The method checks to see if the object is interacting with the Paddle. If it is, then it will call the OnPickUp() method, disable additional collisions by turning off the collider and renderer components, and play a sound while waiting for 2 seconds.

■ **Note**   Please remember to include the 2D versions of the rigidbody and collider objects and not the 3D ones. There are both 2D and 3D versions of the components and methods with the same names so it's easy to make a mistake in the naming without realizing it.

Save your script using the main File menu in MonoDevelop. With the foundation of our power-ups now defined, we can set up our script for our power-up prefabs scripts. These will be the actual scripts attached to our game objects.

Building Base Power-Up Prefab Scripts

When you think about the traditional Break Out games, two of the most popular power-ups are the paddle size change and the addition of extra balls. The paddle size change makes it easier or harder for our player to keep the ball in play while the extra balls extend the life of the player by giving them more opportunity to stay alive.

We will now create the base script for all of our game objects that will have power-ups falling from them.

1. Right-click in the Scripts folder of the Unity Editor and select Create, C# Script.

2. Name the script PowerUpDrop and press Enter.

3. Double-click on the script and change it to match the script in Listing 6-2.

Listing 6-2. Power-Up Prefab script

```
using UnityEngine;
using System.Collections;

[RequireComponent(typeof(BoxCollider2D))]
public class PowerUpDrop : MonoBehaviour {

    public BasePowerUp PowerUpPrefab;
```

```
//OnCollision create the powerup
void OnCollisionEnter2D(Collision2D c)
{
    GameObject.Instantiate(PowerUpPrefab, this.transform.position,
    Quaternion.identity);
}

}
```

If we take a look at this script we see that we start off by requiring a BoxCollider2D component on our object. This ensures that the object will be able to collide with the ball in the scene. Therefore a game object that cannot be destroyed by the ball should not have a power-up attached to it.

Next we include the appropriate power up prefab object to the game object. We have not created our power up prefabs objects yet but will create them shortly. Finally in the OnCollisionEnter2D() method we instantiate or create our prefab object at the current transform position. Using the Quaternion.identity variable means that there is no rotation on the object and it is perfectly aligned with the World space of the game.

We will attach this script to certain brick objects later in the chapter.

Extra Balls Script

The next script, shown in Listing 6-3, will inherit the Power-Up base script. The purpose of the script is for the balls that will fall from our Brick objects. These balls will be the extra balls in the game and will handle the interaction of them in the game.

Listing 6-3. Extra ball prefab script

```
using UnityEngine;
using System.Collections;

public class ExtraBall : BasePowerUp {

    //BallPrefab instantiated when the powerup is picked up
    public GameObject BallPrefab;

    //Make the min and max speed to be configurable in the editor.
    public float MinSpeed = 10;
    public float MaxSpeed = 20;

    //To prevent the ball from keep bouncing horizontally we enforce a
    minimum vertical movement
    public float MinVerticalMovement = 0.5F;
```

```
//Override of the OnPickup method of the base class
protected override void OnPickup()
{
    //Call the default behaviour of the base class first
    base.OnPickup();
    print ("On pickup Call!");
}

void Update () {

}

void OnCollisionEnter2D(Collision2D c)
{
    print ("Extra Collison");

    if (c.gameObject.tag == "Paddle"){
        print ("Extra Collison Paddle");
        launchBall();
    }
}

public void launchBall() {
    //Get current speed and direction
    Vector2 direction = GetComponent<Rigidbody2D>().velocity;
    //float speed = 20f;
    float speed = direction.magnitude;
    direction.Normalize();

    //Make sure the ball never goes straight horizotal else it could
    never come down to the paddle.
    if (direction.x > -MinimumVerticalMovement && direction.x <
    MinimumVerticalMovement)
    {
        //Adjust the x, make sure it goes in a direction within the
        range limit set
        direction.x = direction.x < 0 ? -MinimumVerticalMovement :
        MinimumVerticalMovement;

        //Adjust the y, make sure it keeps going into the direction it
        was going (up or down)
        direction.y = direction.y < 0 ? -1 + MinimumVerticalMovement :
        1 - MinimumVerticalMovement;

        //Apply it back to the ball
        GetComponent<Rigidbody2D>().velocity = direction * speed;
    }
```

```
if (speed < MinimumSpeed || speed > MaximumSpeed)
{
    //Limit the speed so it always above min en below max
    speed = Mathf.Clamp(speed, MinimumSpeed, MaximumSpeed);

    //Apply the limit
    //Note that we don't use * Time.deltaTime here since we set the
    velocity once, not every frame.
    GetComponent<Rigidbody2D>().velocity = direction * speed;
}

}
}
```

Let's walk through the script. First we define the variables for the minimum/ maximum speed and vertical movement of the ball. The next major section in the script is the OnCollisionEnter2D() method that will handle the collision of the object. The first thing the method checks for is that the collision is happening with the Paddle. We don't want the ball to react unless it is hitting the Paddle.

Once this is confirmed, we call the launchBall() method in order to set the direction that the ball will launch in. We want the direction to be random and at an angle so the ball doesn't react the same every time. This will make the game less predictable and harder for the player of the game. The launchBall() method grabs the information on the rigidbody component and then sets a variable for the speed using the magnitude of the object's direction.

■ **Note**   Want to learn more about the meaning of Vector object math? Check out Understanding Vector Arithmetic in the Unity Manual here: http://docs.unity3d.com/ Manual/UnderstandingVectorArithmetic.html.

Next we ensure the direction of the ball is set at an angle that is within the minimum and maximum values we have defined for the ball. The variables are public so they can be customized for the ball in the Inspector View. One important thing to notice in our script is that we use something called the ternary operator to define this condition. For example, we set the direction of x using the following ternary operator:

```
direction.x = direction.x < 0 ? -MinimumVerticalMovement :
MinimumVerticalMovement;
```

The first part of the condition we check is the Boolean condition or true or false. This is the direction.x<0 portion of the script. If this test is true we set direction.x to negative MinimumVerticalMovement. If it is false we just set it to the value of the variable. Using a ternary operator instead of the if/then statement reduces the number of lines of code in our scripts.

We also make sure the speed of the ball is limited as well to a specific value. Every time the ball has a collision with our `Paddle`, the ball will be launched at a velocity within the minimum and maximum values.

Click Save on the MonoDevelop File menu and return to the Unity Editor. Before we use the Extra Ball script we will need to modify our Ball script. Navigate to the Assets folder and find the Scripts folder. Select the Ball Script and modify it to match the details in Listing 6-4.

Listing 6-4. Ball script modified

```
using UnityEngine;
using System.Collections;

public class Ball : MonoBehaviour {

    public Paddle paddle;
    public bool gameStarted = false;
    private Vector3 paddleVector;

    //Make the min and max speed to be configurable in the editor.
    public float MinimumSpeed = 10;
    public float MaximumSpeed = 20;

    //To prevent the ball from keep bouncing horizontally we enforce a
    minimum vertical movement
    public float MinimumVerticalMovement = 0.5F;

    // Use this for initialization
    void Start () {
        //Set the ball on the paddle position
        paddleVector = this.transform.position - paddle.transform.position;
    }

    // Update is called once per frame
    void Update () {
        if(!gameStarted){
            this.transform.position = paddle.transform.position +
            paddleVector;
                if(Input.GetMouseButtonDown(0)){
                    print("Mouse clicked!");
                    gameStarted = true;
                    this.GetComponent<Rigidbody2D>().velocity = new Vector2
                    (Random.Range(-2.0f, 2.0f),10f);
                }
        }
        launchBall ();
    }
```

```
public void launchBall() {
    //Get current speed and direction
    Vector2 direction = GetComponent<Rigidbody2D>().velocity;
    //float speed = 20f;
    float speed = direction.magnitude;
    direction.Normalize();

    //Make sure the ball never goes straight horizotal else it could
    never come down to the paddle.
    if (direction.x > -MinimumVerticalMovement && direction.x <
    MinimumVerticalMovement)
    {

        //Adjust the x to limit it to the movement left or right
        direction.x = direction.x < 0 ? -MinimumVerticalMovement :
        MinimumVerticalMovement;

        //Adjust the y, make sure it keeps going into the direction it
        was going (up or down)
        direction.y = direction.y < 0 ? -1 + MinimumVerticalMovement :
        1 - MinimumVerticalMovement;

        //print(direction.x);

        //Apply it back to the ball
        GetComponent<Rigidbody2D>().velocity = direction * speed;
    }

    if (speed < MinimumSpeed || speed > MaximumSpeed)
    {
        //Limit the speed so it always above min en below max
        speed = Mathf.Clamp(speed, MinimumSpeed, MaximumSpeed);

        //Apply the limit
        //Note that we don't use * Time.deltaTime here since we set the
        velocity once, not every frame.
        GetComponent<Rigidbody2D>().velocity = direction * speed;
    }

}
}
```

Our script will be very similar to the Extra Ball script now. Really the main difference is the starting point where we place our ball on the paddle in the Start() method. Now with our Ball and Extra Ball prefab scripts set, let's add a script for modifying Paddle size.

Change Paddle Size Script

Resizing the paddle is another feature of the game that adds interactivity and fun. Making a larger paddle reduces the odds that the player will not lose their ball off the screen, while making it small increases the odds. Let's extend the BasePowerUp class we have with a script to make the paddle modifications.

1. While in the Unity Editor, navigate to the Assets, Scripts folder.

2. Right-click and select Create, C# Script to add a new script to the folder.

3. Name the script "ChangePaddleSize" and press enter.

4. Double-click on the created script and change it to match the script in Listing 6-5.

Listing 6-5. Change Paddle Size script

```csharp
using UnityEngine;
using System.Collections;

public class ChangePaddleSize : BasePowerUp
{
    //How much units should the paddle change when this powerup is picked up?
    //Can also be negative to shrink the paddle!
    public Vector3 SizeIncrease = Vector3.zero;

    public Vector3 MinPaddleSize = new Vector3(0.1F, 0.1F, 0.4F);

    //Notice how we override we the OnPickup method of the base class
    protected override void OnPickup()
    {
        //Call the default behaviour of the base class first
        base.OnPickup();

        //Then do the powerup specific behaviour, changing the size in this case
        Paddle p = FindObjectOfType(typeof(Paddle)) as Paddle;
        p.transform.localScale += SizeIncrease;

        //Limit the minimal size of the paddle
        Vector3 size = p.transform.localScale;
        if (size.x < MinPaddleSize.x) {
            size.x = MinPaddleSize.x;
        }
```

```
      if (size.y < MinPaddleSize.y) {
          size.y = MinPaddleSize.y;
      }

      if (size.z < MinPaddleSize.z) {
          size.z = MinPaddleSize.z;
      }

      p.transform.localScale = size;
   }
}
```

The Change Paddle Size script starts off by extending the BasePowerUp script that we created earlier in this chapter. Next it defines two public variables that we can modify through the Inspector View of our prefab object. The SizeIncrease and MinimumPaddleSize variables will define by how much our paddle increases or decreases in size when the power-up is engaged.

Next we override the OnPickUp() method from the BasePowerUp class, search for the object of type Paddle in our scene, and transform it. We set the localScale of the object to the new Vector 3 size after we define it. Save the script by using the File Menu in MonoDevelop.

Ok, that was a lot of creating and changing scripts. Let's go back to the Unity Editor now to view some of the fruits of our labor.

Creating Prefab Game Objects for Ball and Paddle Changes

In our Unity Editor we should see all scripts defined in our Scripts folder under Assets. Figure 6-1 shows the scripts we should have available.

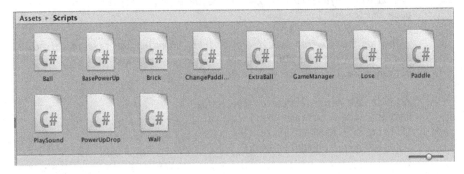

Figure 6-1. Script list in the Assets folder

Now we will use the `ExtraBall` and `ChangePaddleSize` scripts in our prefabs that we will drop in our scene. We begin with the extra ball addition.

Sprites for Prefabs

In order to add the prefab objects to our project, we need to include the sprites for each of the Power-Ups. Navigate to the project files and find the shrinkarrow, `growarrow`, and `ball_04` images to the Sprites folder. Your Sprites folder should now look like Figure 6-2.

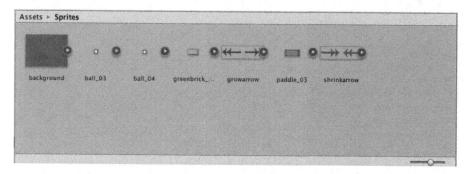

Figure 6-2. *List of sprites in the Assets, Sprites folder*

Select `ball_04` of the Sprites and navigate to the Inspector View. Change the Pixels per unit from 100 to 50 so that it matches the `ball_03` sprite. With our sprites in the project, we can build the prefabs we need for our game.

Extra Ball Prefab

To build the Prefab for the Extra Ball, we will start with the existing Ball Prefab that we have in our project. Navigate to the Assets, Prefab folder. Select the Ball prefab object that you created, click on the Edit button from the main Unity menu and select Duplicate. Click the name of the duplicate object and rename it to "ExtraBall."

In the Inspector View, let's change the sprite to the new sprite we just imported. Select the circle next to the Sprite and choose `ball_04` from the selection window. Next add an Audio Source component to the object by clicking Add Component, selecting Audio, and selecting Audio Source.

Next add the ExtraBall script that we created by selecting Add Component, Scripts, and choosing the ExtraBall script. Modify the settings to match Figure 6-3 where Drop Speed is 5, Minimum Speed is 10, Maximum Speed is 20, and Minimum Vertical Movement is 0.6.

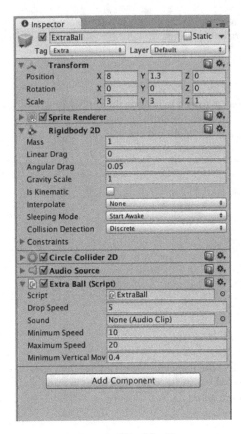

Figure 6-3. ExtraBall Prefab object

Next let's create the prefabs for modifying our Paddle.

Shrink and Grow Prefabs

The shrink and grow prefab objects will be used to increase and decrease the size of our paddle. Let's build the prefab objects using the sprites that we imported. First navigate to the Sprites folder under Assets to the growarrow and shrinkarrow sprites. Select both sprites and drag then into the Hierarchy View. Next drag them from the Hierarchy View down to the Assets, Prefab folder. This will convert them into prefab objects. Finally delete the two objects from the Hierarchy View. Now you should have a Prefab folder that looks like Figure 6-4 with 5 prefab objects.

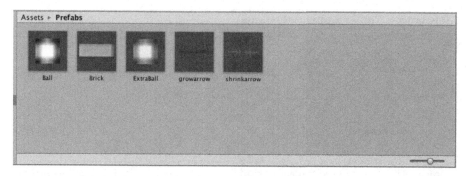

Figure 6-4. *List of prefab objects*

We will need to modify both the growarrow and shrinkarrow prefabs to include the components that we need. Starting with the growarrow, select the prefab object. In the Inspector View click the Add Component button, select Physics2D, and select RigidBody2D.

Next repeat the same steps but select BoxCollider2D. This will add the collision component that the object needs to interact with the paddle after it drops. Next add the audio component by selecting Add Component, Audio and select Audio Source.

Finally add the ChangePaddleSize script to the growarrow prefab by selecting Add Component, Scripts, and selecting the script. Modify the attributes to have a Drop Speed of 2; Size settings of X=0.7, Y=0.1, Z=0; and Min Paddle Size settings of X=0.1, Y=0.1, and Z=0.4. After all is complete, your prefab should look like Figure 6-5.

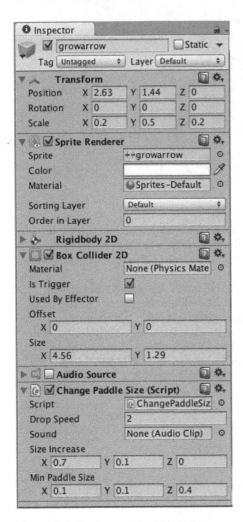

Figure 6-5. *Growarrow Prefab attributes*

For the shrinkarrow prefab simply repeat the steps. However set the attributes of the ChangePaddleSize script for the Size settings to X=-0.7, Y=-0.1, Z=0. This will reduce the paddle instead of increasing it since the values are negative.

All of our prefab objects are now built and we are ready to set up our scene. Select File and Save Scene from the main Unity menu to save what we have created.

Putting it All Together in the Scene

Our prefab objects are complete so we can make our bricks more interactive. First let's add two more rows of bricks to our scene. In the Hierarchy View collapse, the Bricks game object that contains our row of bricks. Right-click on the name and select Duplicate. Rename the created duplicate from Bricks(1) to Bricks Row 2. Duplicate the step again and rename the create object to Bricks Row 3. In the Inspector View, set Transform Position Y to 6.5 for the Bricks Row 2 object and Transform Position Y to 7 for Bricks Row 3. Our scene should now look like Figure 6-6.

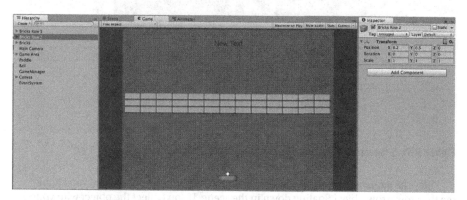

Figure 6-6. *New Brick Rows*

Press play in the Game View. The game should play as it did before. Stop the game and choose the third Brick object under the Bricks game object. Click Add Component, select Script, and add the PowerUpDrop script. In the Project View under the Prefabs folder, select the growarrow prefab and drag/drop it in the Inspector View under Power-Up Prefab attribute of the ChangePaddleSize script (Figure 6-7).

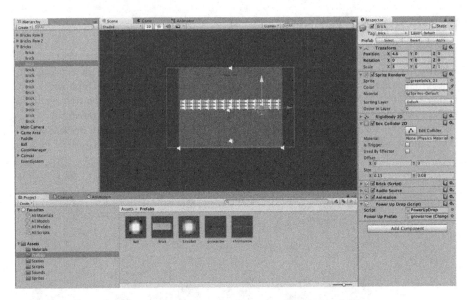

Figure 6-7. *Selected Brick game object with ChangePaddleSize prefab*

Play the game and try to hit the Brick with the ball. When you succeed you should see the growarrow object floating down in the scene. If you collect the object with your paddle, the paddle will increase in size (Figure 6-8).

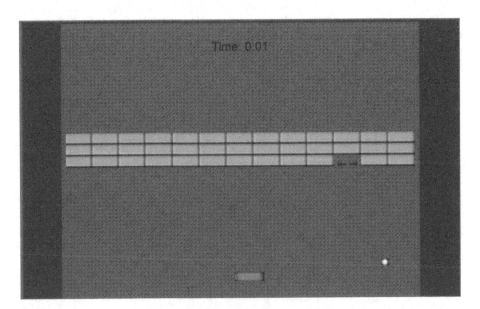

Figure 6-8. *Growarrow prefab falling after brick was hit by ball*

You can randomly add the PowerUpDrop script to Brick objects on each of the three rows. Mix it up by adding ExtraBall, growarrow, and shrinkarrow prefabs to the Power-Up Prefab attribute of the components.

Modify the Lose Script

Finally let's make a slight modification to our Lose script (see Listing 6-6). We will instruct our script to only trigger the lose routine if the object passing through it is a Ball.

Listing 6-6. Lose Script

```
using UnityEngine;
using System.Collections;

public class Lose : MonoBehaviour {
    private Ball ball;
    private GameManager gameManager;

    IEnumerator Pause() {
        print("Before Waiting 2 seconds");
        //Switch GameManager State
        gameManager = GameObject.FindObjectOfType<GameManager>();
        gameManager.SwitchState (GameState.Failed);
        gameManager.ChangeText ("You Lose :(");

        yield return new WaitForSeconds(2);

        //Find the ball and reset game start
        ball = GameObject.FindObjectOfType<Ball>();
        ball.gameStarted = false;

        //Reload level
        Application.LoadLevel(Application.loadedLevel);

        print("After Waiting 2 Seconds");
    }

    void OnTriggerEnter2D (Collider2D trigger){
        if (trigger.name == "Ball") {
            print ("Lost Triggered!");

            //Wait before restarting level
            StartCoroutine (Pause ());
        }
    }
}
```

When we play our game now the prefab power-up objects will fall through the bottom without impacting the game play.

Summary

In this chapter we added power-up objects and scripts to our game. We set up scripts on our bricks objects to allow the release of power-up prefab objects on collision with our ball. In addition we updated our Lose script to only end the game when the ball object interacts with it.

▮ **Note** Our current Lose script will end when the main ball object passes through. However we don't want our game to end if there are extra balls still alive. We will solve this in the next chapter.

In the next chapter we will add some final touches to the game. In addition we will add additional Scenes and develop a basic user menu.

Just because something doesn't do what you planned it to do doesn't mean it's useless.

—Thomas Edison

■ ■ ■

CHAPTER 7

Level Manager and Menu

Controlling the flow of the game when a user plays involves many important decisions. For example, do you want the user to navigate through the levels themselves, or do you want to force them into specific levels? Can the user retain their progress through the game or will they be forced to start over every time? Will the high score be retained by the game and shown to the next player? These and other game design decisions impact how your game is perceived by players and whether it is an easy, enjoyable experience for your game player.

In this chapter we will design the game object that controls the level navigation. In addition we will create a Menu for our user to select which level that they want to play. We will also force the user to the main game menu when they complete the level (i.e., win).

Let's get leveled up!

Creating Intro Scene

After the splash scene is loaded for the game, the first, or introductory, scene is what your user will see. Right now our game goes straight into the Main level of our game. We will change this and have the user see a menu scene first when they enter the game.

Let's begin by creating a new scene in Unity. Select the Assets, Scenes folder in the Hierarchy View. From the main Unity menu select File and then the New Scene option. This will create the scene we will use for building our Menu. Select File again and then the Save Scene As option. Name the Scene Intro and Save it to the Scenes folder under Assets.

Add a Main Title and Buttons

In the Using UI text to Display Information in Chapter 4, we learned how to create a UI Text object to display text information. We will follow similar steps here to create our main title text for the Intro scene. Select GameObject, UI, Text (Figure 7-1) from the main Unity menu.

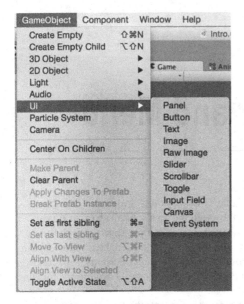

Figure 7-1. Gameobject selection for creating a new Canvas UI Text object

This will create a new Canvas option in the Hierarchy View of the scene. You should also see under the Canvas object a Text object containing the text "New Text" as you saw in Chapter 4. Modify the Canvas object by selecting it and navigating to the Inspector View. Change the name in the Inspector to "Title." In the Text (Script) component, change the text to "BREAK THOSE BRICKS," set the Font Size to 35, and both the Horizontal and Vertical Overflow to "Overflow."

Next modify the Rect Transform Width to 440 and Height to 58. Alter the positions yo Pos X = 0, Pos Y = 163, and Pos Z = 0. Make sure the paragraph alignment is center so the title text is always in the middle of the screen.

Your Canvas component should now match Figure 7-2, and we should see our text in the middle of the screen like Figure 7-3. Save your scene using the main Unity menu and selecting Save Scene.

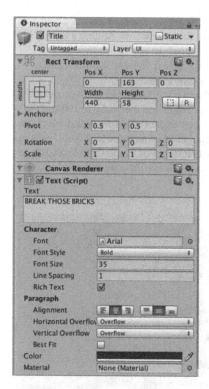

Figure 7-2. *Canvas Title object*

Figure 7-3. *Break those bricks title text in Game View*

117

Next we will need to add some buttons to our title screen. The buttons will allow our game player to navigate to the levels that we want them to access. Adding a button is relatively simple since we have our Canvas already defined. To add a button we just select Gameobject, UI, and select Button from the main Unity menu. Select the button and change the name of it to "Level 1 Button" in the Inspector View.

Now let's modify the attributes of the button so that it is in the right location on our screen. In the Inspector View of the button, change the Height and the Width to 100 and the Pos X = -209, Pos Y=50, and Pos Z=0. In the Hierarchy View expand the Button and select the text. In the Inspector View change the Text (Script) component Text attribute to "Level 1." Set the Font Size to 14. Modify the Rect Transform and set the Left, Top, Pos Z, and Right to 0. Change the Bottom attribute to 50. Figure 7-4 below shows what our Scene View should now look like.

Figure 7-4. Level 1 button in Scene View of Canvas object

One of the great features of using the UI Canvas system that Unity has included is that it has an EventSystem built in to handle input, raycasting, and sending events. We will use this system to handle our button interaction so we don't need to code our buttons ourselves. However we do need to script what the button will do once it is clicked. Let's add a level loader script to load the specified level on button click.

Script for Loading a Level

Unity makes it easy for us to add interactivity to our button using the UI elements. However we still need to add our own custom method to accept a level number passed in and then load the scene. Navigate to the Assets, Scripts folder to create a new script.

Right-click in the folder and select Create, C# Script. Name the script LevelLoader, and double-click to modify it to the script in Listing 7-1.

Listing 7-1. LevelLoader script used for loading the specified level

```
using UnityEngine;
using System.Collections;

public class LevelLoader : MonoBehaviour {

//Basic function for loading level
    public void LoadScene (int level)
        {
            Application.LoadLevel(level);
        }
}
```

In the script we set a LoadScene() method that takes the integer of the level to be loaded. Right now we only have once level created, but we will create three more shortly. We use the LoadLevel() method of Application provided by the Unity libraries to move our user to the defined scene. Save the script in MonoDevelop and return to the Unity Editor.

Select the Canvas object and drag/drop the LevelLoader script in the objects Inspector View (Figure 7-5).

Figure 7-5. Level Loader script added to the Canvas object

Under the Inspector View of our button under the Button (Script) component there is an OnClick section. To interact with the Canvas we created we will need to add the object under this section. Click the plus button to add an object that will run at runtime. From the Hierarchy View, drag the Canvas object to the space under the Runtime Only drop-down option. In the drop-down on the right, search for and find the LoadScene() method you just created. Select it and change the number from 0 to 1 (Figure 7-6).

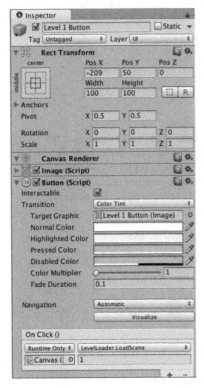

Figure 7-6. *Level 1 Button with Canvas in On Click() method*

■ **Note**   If the LoadScene() method is not visible, try refreshing your script folder and verify that the method is defined as public void. Also make sure the there is no text showing up as red in Monodevelop. An error will stop the method from showing up in the list. This includes misspellings and case issues. Verifying the code status in the Unity Editor Console View will help identify any errors as well

---

We are now set with our button. Since we have an Intro scene, let's modify our level scene to handle our Lose scenario better.

Modifying the Game Lose Scenario

In Chapter 4 we scripted our Lose Collider to automatically restart the level when a player misses the ball. The Lose Collider triggers the level to restart using the ApplicationLoadLevel() method. In this section we modify the game to present the player button options to restart the level or return to the main scene. This makes the game more user friendly since they aren't forced to restart a level they don't want to play again. In addition it allows them to escape the scene since the current game play does not allow for that.

Let's begin by modifying our Canvas first. Select the Canvas in the Hierarchy View. In the Project View navigate to the Assets, Scripts folder to find the LevelLoader script we created earlier in the chapter. Drag and drop that script into the Inspector View of the Canvas object. This will allow us to reference this script when we define our buttons for the scene.

Add Restart and Main Menu Buttons

Next on the main Unity Editor menu select GameObject, UI, Button. This will add a button to our scene and automatically place it in our existing Canvas. With the Scene View tab visible, double-click on the Canvas object in the Hierarchy View so we can see where the new button is located. Select the button under the Canvas in the Hierarchy View and rename it to "Restart" by modifying the name of the object at the top in the Inspector View. Under the Rect Transform section set the Pos X = 1.5, Pos Y = 0, and Pos Z = 0. This will center the button in our scene over the bricks.

Now select the Text object under the Button in the Hierarchy View. In the Inspector of the Text object rename the Text (Script) text to "Restart." In the On Click() section, click the plus sign and then drag/drop the Canvas object from the Hierarchy View to the object section under the Runtime Only drop-down. Since we are restarting Level 1, change the value to 1.

Repeat the steps to build a "Main Menu" button. For this button set the name to "MainMenu," the Rect Transform section set the Pos X = 1.5, Pos Y = -41, and Pos Z = 0, the text to "Main Menu," and the Load Level number to 0.

Add a Panel for the Buttons

Adding a Panel to the scene will provide a visual overlay on top of our bricks for the buttons. This helps add a level of separation for the buttons and helps the user see that an action by them is required to continue. On the main Unity Editor menu select GameObject, UI, Panel. This will create a Panel object under our Canvas in the Hierarchy View that covers our entire Canvas. Select the Panel object and modify the Rect Transform attribute in the Inspector View to Left = 152.5, Top = 124, Pos Z = 0, Right = 152.5, and Bottom = 102.

If you look at the Scene View after double-clicking the Game Area in the Hierarchy View you should see the Panel overlaying the bricks in our scene (Figure 7-7).

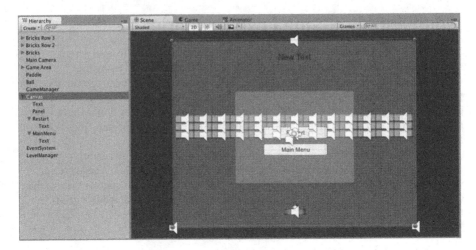

Figure 7-7. *Panel view with buttons on Canvas object*

In the Inspector View for the Panel, Restart, and MainMenu objects, disable them by unchecking the check box next to their names. We will use scripting to enable the objects since we want them only to appear when the lose scenario occurs.

Updating the GameManager and Lose Scripts

The GameManager script we created in Chapter 4 will need to be updated to enable our Canvas objects. In the Project View, navigate to the Assets, Scripts folder and double-click the GameManager script. Modify the script in MonoDevelop to match the script in Listing 7-2.

Listing 7-2. Updated GameManager script for showing Canvas objects

```
using UnityEngine;
using System.Collections;
using UnityEngine.UI;

//List of all the possible gamestates
public enum GameState
{
    NotStarted,
    Playing,
    Completed,
    Failed
}
//Require an audio source for the object
[RequireComponent(typeof(AudioSource))]
```

```csharp
public class GameManager : MonoBehaviour {

    //Sounds to be played when entering one of the gamestates
    public AudioClip StartSound;
    public AudioClip FailedSound;

    private GameState currentState = GameState.NotStarted;

    //All the blocks found in this level, to keep track of how many are left
    private Brick[] allBricks;
    private Ball[] allBalls;
    private Paddle paddle;

    public float Timer=0.0f;
    private int minutes;
    private int seconds;
    public string formattedTime;

    private Text feedback;
    public Text text;

    public GameObject restartButton;
    public GameObject mainMenuButton;
    public GameObject buttonBackground;

    // Use this for initialization
    void Start () {

        Time.timeScale=1;

        //Find all the blocks in this scene
        allBricks = FindObjectsOfType(typeof(Brick)) as Brick[];

        //Find all the balls in this scene
        allBalls = FindObjectsOfType(typeof(Ball)) as Ball[];

        paddle = GameObject.FindObjectOfType<Paddle>();

        print ("Bricks:" + allBricks.Length);
        print ("Balls:" + allBalls.Length);
        print ("Paddle" + paddle);

        //Change start text
        ChangeText ("Click To Begin");

        //Prepare the start of the level
        SwitchState(GameState.NotStarted);

    }
```

```
// Update is called once per frame
void Update () {

    switch (currentState)
    {
    case GameState.NotStarted:
        //Change start text
        ChangeText ("Click To Begin");
        //Check if the player taps/clicks.
        if (Input.GetMouseButtonDown(0))        //Note: on mobile this will
                                                 translate to the first
                                                 touch/finger so perfectly
                                                 multiplatform!

        {
            SwitchState(GameState.Playing);
        }
        break;

    case GameState.Playing:
    {

        Timer += Time.deltaTime;
        minutes= Mathf.FloorToInt(Timer/60F);
        seconds= Mathf.FloorToInt(Timer-minutes *60);
        formattedTime=string.Format("{0:0}:{1:00}", minutes, seconds);

        ChangeText ("Time: "+formattedTime);

        bool allBlocksDestroyed = false;

        //Are there no balls left?
        if (FindObjectOfType(typeof(Ball)) == null)
            SwitchState(GameState.Failed);

        if (allBlocksDestroyed)
            SwitchState(GameState.Completed);
    }
        break;
        //Both cases do the same: restart the game
    case GameState.Failed:
        print ("Gamestate Failed!");
        ChangeText ("You Lose :(");
            break;
    case GameState.Completed:
        bool allBlocksDestroyedFinal = false;

        //Destroy all the balls and extra balls
        Ball[] others = FindObjectsOfType(typeof(Ball)) as Ball[];
```

```
        foreach(Ball other in others) {
            Destroy(other.gameObject);
        }
        break;
    }

}

public void EnableButtons () {
    //Enable buttons for when the player loses
    restartButton.SetActive (true);
    mainMenuButton.SetActive (true);
    buttonBackground.SetActive (true);
}

public void ChangeText (string text) {
    //Find Canvas and modify text
    GameObject canvas = GameObject.Find("Canvas");
    Text[] textValue = canvas.GetComponentsInChildren<Text>();
    textValue[0].text = text;
}

public void SwitchState(GameState newState)
{
    currentState = newState;

    switch (currentState)
    {
    default:
    case GameState.NotStarted:
        break;

    case GameState.Playing:
        GetComponent<AudioSource>().PlayOneShot(StartSound);
        break;

    case GameState.Completed:
        GetComponent<AudioSource>().PlayOneShot(StartSound);
        break;

    case GameState.Failed:
        GetComponent<AudioSource>().PlayOneShot(FailedSound);
        break;
    }
}

}
```

The key changes to the script are highlighted. We added variables for the MainMenu button, Restart button, and Panel. Then we added a method called EnableButtons() for enabling the objects that we can call from our Lose script. Save the script.

Next it's time to change the Lose script to utilize the Canvas objects we just created. In the Project View, navigate to the Assets, Scripts folder and double-click the Lose script. Modify the script in MonoDevelop to match the script in Listing 7-3.

Listing 7-3. Updated Lose script for showing Canvas objects

```
using UnityEngine;
using System.Collections;

public class Lose : MonoBehaviour {
    private Ball ball;
    private GameManager gameManager;
    public GameObject[] players;
    public GameObject[] extras;

    IEnumerator Pause() {
        print("Before Waiting 2 seconds");
        //Switch GameManager State
        gameManager = GameObject.FindObjectOfType<GameManager>();
        gameManager.SwitchState (GameState.Failed);

        //enable the restart and main menu buttons
        gameManager.EnableButtons();

        yield return new WaitForSeconds(2);

        print("After Waiting 2 Seconds");
    }

        void OnTriggerEnter2D (Collider2D trigger){
        if (trigger.name == "Ball") {
            print ("Lost Triggered!");

            //Wait before restarting level
            StartCoroutine (Pause ());
        }
    }

}
```

Our Lose script now will call our GameManager to enable the buttons instead of restarting our level.

Finally in the Unity Editor refresh the Scripts folder under the Project View. In the Hierarchy View select the GameManager object. You should now see options for the three public variables that we created. Drag and drop the Panel, Restart button, and MainMenu button into the appropriate areas in the Inspector View of the GameManager Script component (Figure 7-8).

▼ ⓒ ☑ Game Manager (Script)		🖻 ⚙︎▾
Script	◉ GameManager	◎
Start Sound	🐾 game-started	◎
Failed Sound	🐾 game-ended	◎
Timer	0	
Formatted Time		
Text	None (Text)	◉
Restart Button	Restart	◉
Main Menu Button	MainMenu	◉
Button Background	Panel	◉

Figure 7-8. GameManager object with the Canvas objects included

Save the scene and press Play in the Game View to review the scene. When you miss the ball you will see the menu we created instead of the level restarting (Figure 7-9).

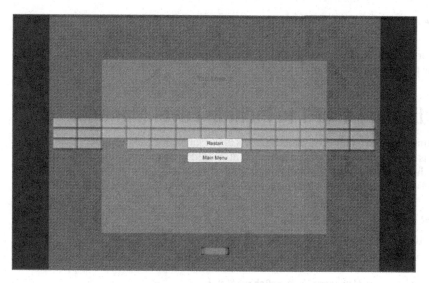

Figure 7-9. Menu screen with options to restart or go to main menu

127

Rename and Duplicate Main Scene

The main level of our game is currently defined in our Scenes folder as Main. We are now going to create multiple levels for our game so we need a more uniform naming convention for our Scenes. Let's go ahead and rename our Main scene to a level name that makes sense for our game. In the Assets, Scenes folder, single-click the text of the Main scene. This should make the text editable. Change the text to "Level1" and hit Enter.

Now with our Scene named correctly, let's create three more that we will map buttons to. Select the Level1 scene. On the main Unity menu select Edit, Duplicate. Unity will duplicate our scene and automatically increment the number for you to 2. Repeat the process until you have four scenes in your Scenes folder along with your Intro scene (Figure 7-10).

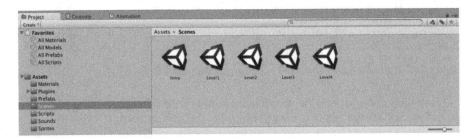

Figure 7-10. *Level Scenes with Intro Scene in folder*

For now this is all that we need to do. We will modify the scenes later to make them unique for each level.

Modifying Level 1 to Include Level Manager

To manage the navigation between the levels in our game, we will need more than the buttons in our Intro level. Game players will also need to be redirected to the main scene when they complete the level by eliminating all of the bricks. Let's create a script called LevelManager to control how our player will move between the scenes (see Listing 7-4).

Listing 7-4. Level Manager Script

```
using UnityEngine;
using System.Collections;

public class LevelManager : MonoBehaviour {

    public GameObject[] bricks;
    public int count=0;
    private GameManager gameManager;
    public string FinishTime;
```

```
    // Use this for initialization
    void Start () {

    }

    // Update is called once per frame
    void Update () {
        bricks = GameObject.FindGameObjectsWithTag ("Brick");
        Debug.Log("Brick Count: "+bricks.Length);
        count = bricks.Length;

        if (count == 0) {
            Debug.Log("All bricks are gone!");

            //Wait before returning to Main level
            StartCoroutine (Pause ());

        }

    }

IEnumerator Pause() {
    print("Before Waiting 5 seconds");
    //Switch GameManager State
    gameManager = GameObject.FindObjectOfType<GameManager>();
    gameManager.SwitchState (GameState.Completed);
    gameManager.ChangeText ("You Win :)");
    FinishTime = gameManager.formattedTime;

    Debug.Log("Took "+FinishTime+ " to finish the game");

    yield return new WaitForSeconds(5);

    //Reload Main Menu
    LoadScene (0);
    print("After Waiting 5 Seconds went to main menu");
}

    public void LoadScene (int level)
    {
        Application.LoadLevel(level);
    }
}
```

In this script we start by defining public objects for our bricks, count, and finish time. We will use these variables to track how many bricks we have left in our scene and how long it takes us to clear the level. We will use this information of the game play in the future to identify the players who are the best in finishing particular levels and possibly for adding game play performance stars to our levels.

Next we set our Update script to constantly check for the number of bricks left in our scene. We search for objects labeled with the tag of Brick and update our count with the number. When the count reaches zero we begin our Pause() method defined later in the script.

Next we set up our Pause() method. The method will search for the GameManager object we defined earlier in the book. It will call the SwitchState() method and pass the GameState.Completed enumerator to set the game as completed. Calling this method will destroy the main ball object we have left in our scene. We then switch the text in the scene from the timer countdown to the "You Win :)" text and save the formattedTime variable to the FinishTime variable. We display this for 5 seconds then make the call to load our Intro Scene we defined as scene 0 in our Build Settings.

■ **Note**   Now is a good time to verify your Brick prefab and Paddle object to make sure they are tagged appropriately in the Inspector View. Both should be tagged appropriately as Brick and Paddle, respectively.

Adding Scenes to the Build Settings

Ok, we have our scenes and our one-button setup. However, running the game and pressing the button now will not do anything in our game. In order for the scene to load, Unity needs to know what levels are available in the game and that needs to be defined in our Build Settings area. This area can be found under File in the Unity Editor menu. Select Build settings to view the scene definition in the Scenes In Build section.

To add our scene to the settings area, we need to open each of the scenes we created and click the Add Current button. All the scenes should show up in the Scenes In Build section now (Figure 7-11).

Figure 7-11. *Build Settings with Scenes in Build section*

Press the Play button in the Game View to test your Intro scene. You should now be able to click the Level 1 button. On click you should be taken to the Level 1 scene.

___

■ **Note**   If the Scenes are not in the right order, just drag and drop them in the Scenes In Build window. You can delete scenes by hitting the delete button with the selected scene as well.

___

Add Additional Buttons

Without scenes defined in the settings, we can add additional buttons to our Intro scene. In the Hierarchy View, select the Level 1 button, right-click on it, and select Duplicate. Rename the button to Level 2, change the text to match, and set the On Click() number to 2. Repeat the process for levels 3 and 4, setting the attributes for each according to Table 7-1.

Table 7-1. *Button Settings*

Button	Rec Transform Attributes
1	Pos X = -209 Pos Y = 50 Pos Z = 0 Width = 100 Height = 100
2	Pos X = -76 Pos Y = 50 Pos Z = 0 Width = 100 Height = 100
3	Pos X = 76 Pos Y = 50 Pos Z = 0 Width = 100 Height = 100
4	Pos X = 212 Pos Y = 50 Pos Z = 0 Width = 100 Height = 100

One more thing we want to do before testing the game is to change the background color of our intro scene. Select the main camera object in the Hierarchy View. In the Inspector View under the Camera component change the Clear Flags from Skybox to Solid Color and select the Background color. Change the hex color to #31793105 so that our scene now has a green background (Figure 7-12).

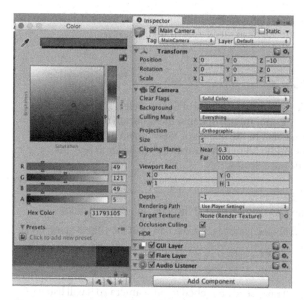

Figure 7-12. *Hex color change for Intro scene background*

Test your game in the Game View (Figure 7-13) and make sure each button navigates to the appropriate level scene.

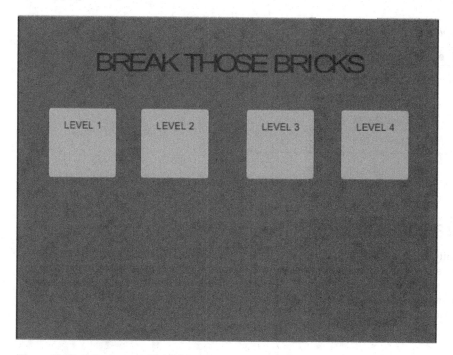

Figure 7-13. *Intro scene with all buttons*

Great! We have the ability to move between levels from the intro Scene. Click Save Project and Save Scene to make sure we have saved everything.

Background Music

In the Intro Scene we will add background music for our Scene. Select GameObject, Create Empty from the main Unity Editor menu. Rename the object in the Hierarchy View to Background Music and select it. In the Inspector View, select Add Component and choose Audio Source. Set the Audio Source to "introBGM" in order to play the background music created for our Intro Scene.

■ **Note**   The music for the game was created by D. J. Twoods. You can find more soundtracks to buy on his web site at `www.gametrackpros.com` or in the iTunes store in the ringtones section.

The AudioListener for the scene is already attached to our camera so it will listen for the sound to play. Press Play in the Game View and we should hear our music. Click on the Level 1 button and the music will change to the sounds we defined for the Level in the GameManager Audio source. Change each GameManager audio source to match Table 7-2.

Table 7-2. *Audio Source Settings*

Level	GameManager Audio Source
1	Level1BGM
2	Level2BGM
3	Level3BGM
4	Level4BGM

When we play our game now, we have different music for each level we choose.

Trailing Ball Effect

Unity has some built-in features we can use to create effects in our game. The Particle System and Trail Renderer options allow for some cool effects to be added to the game. In this section we will add a simple Trail Renderer to our Ball that will create a trailing effect behind the ball as it bounces. The trail can be used to give a visual element of speed and some color as the ball travels.

To add it to our Ball object, select Add Component, Effects, and Trail Renderer in the Inspector View. Modify the Trail Renderer Time, Start Width and End Width attributes to 0.5, 0, and 0.1, respectively. Disable the Trail Renderer component by deselecting the checkbox next to it in the Inspector View. Last, modify the Ball script to the following line in bold in Listing 7-5.

Listing 7-5. Ball script updated to enable Trail Renderer

```
using UnityEngine;
using System.Collections;

public class Ball : MonoBehaviour {

    public Paddle paddle;
    public bool gameStarted = false;
    private Vector3 paddleVector;

    //Make the min and max speed to be configurable in the editor.
    public float MinimumSpeed = 10;
    public float MaximumSpeed = 20;

    //To prevent the ball from keep bouncing horizontally we enforce a
    minimum vertical movement
    public float MinimumVerticalMovement = 0.5F;

    // Use this for initialization
    void Start () {
        //Set the ball on the paddle position
        paddleVector = this.transform.position - paddle.transform.position;
    }

    // Update is called once per frame
    void Update () {
        if(!gameStarted){
            this.transform.position = paddle.transform.position + paddleVector;
                if(Input.GetMouseButtonDown(0)){
                    print("Mouse clicked!");
                    gameStarted = true;
                    this.GetComponent<Rigidbody2D>().velocity = new Vector2
                    (Random.Range(-2.0f, 2.0f),10f);
                    this.GetComponent<TrailRenderer>().enabled = true;
                }
        }
        launchBall ();
    }
```

```
public void launchBall() {
    //Get current speed and direction
    Vector2 direction = GetComponent<Rigidbody2D>().velocity;
    //float speed = 20f;
    float speed = direction.magnitude;
    direction.Normalize();

    //Make sure the ball never goes straight horizotal else it could
    never come down to the paddle.
    if (direction.x > -MinimumVerticalMovement && direction.x <
    MinimumVerticalMovement)
    {

        //Adjust the x to limit it to the movement left or right
        direction.x = direction.x < 0 ? -MinimumVerticalMovement :
        MinimumVerticalMovement;

        //Adjust the y, make sure it keeps going into the direction it
        was going (up or down)
        direction.y = direction.y < 0 ? -1 + MinimumVerticalMovement :
        1 - MinimumVerticalMovement;

        //print(direction.x);

        //Apply it back to the ball
        GetComponent<Rigidbody2D>().velocity = direction * speed;
    }

    if (speed < MinimumSpeed || speed > MaximumSpeed)
    {
        //Limit the speed so it always above min en below max
        speed = Mathf.Clamp(speed, MinimumSpeed, MaximumSpeed);

        //Apply the limit
        //Note that we don't use * Time.deltaTime here since we set the
        velocity once, not every frame.
        GetComponent<Rigidbody2D>().velocity = direction * speed;
    }

}
}
```

Save the script in MonoDevelop, refresh the scripts in the Unity Editor, and press Play in the Game View. You should see a tail following your ball that only appears when the game is started (Figure 7-14).

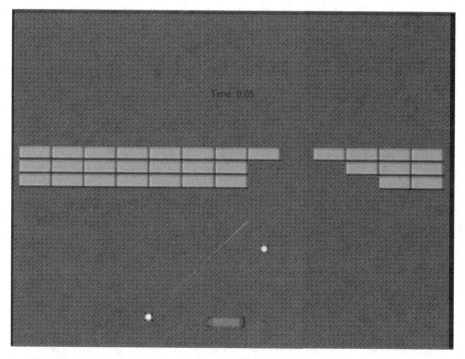

Figure 7-14. Tail following our ball using the Trail Renderer

---

■ **Note**   We are not using the Particle System for our game, but you can view details here
in the Unity Manual at `https://unity3d.com/learn/tutorials/modules/beginner/`
`live-training-archive/particle-systems`

Summary

In this chapter we built our Level Manager for overseeing navigation between the various
levels in our game. We also built a simple menu screen for the players to select which
level that they want to play.

In the next chapter we will build our game using the Unity Cloud. In addition, look at
the different options for deployment across various platforms.

Any sufficiently advanced technology is indistinguishable from magic.

—Arthur C. Clarke, Profiles of the Future:
An Inquiry Into the Limits of the Possible

CHAPTER 8

■ ■ ■

Publishing to the App Store

We have worked hard throughout the book, and now the basics of our game are complete. We have a simple menu system and four levels for our game player to experience. Our game has cool music and power-ups that can be collected to enhance the gaming experience.

In this chapter we will build our game for various platforms including mobile, Web, and desktop. Then we learn how to deploy our game to app stores and build the game using the Unity Cloud.

Time to build and deploy!

Investigating Deployment Options

Unity3d is a cross-platform development tool. It allows for developers to deploy their application on a multitude of supported platforms including desktop, Web, mobile, game console (i.e., Playstation, WiiU, Xbox), Virtual Reality (VR), and Smart TV. Although the options available are numerous, not all of the options are available out of the box with Unity. Some require a special license or version of Unity either directly from the platform manufacturer or from Unity themselves. Below is a table listing information on how to develop Unity for some of the major platform manufacturers.

Table 8-1. *Platform Manufacturers that support Unity deployment*

Platform	Web site
Microsoft XBox	http://www.xbox.com/en-US/Developers
PlayStation	https://www.playstation.com/en-us/develop/
Nintendo WiiU	https://wiiu-developers.nintendo.com
Samsung Smart TV	http://docs.unity3d.com/Manual/samsungtv-gettingstarted.html

For the purpose of this book, we will focus on building our game for the desktop as a stand-alone executable, for the Web in the recently released WebGL format and as an Android app using the Unity Cloud.

Defining Build Settings

To build our game for deployment, we start by viewing and modifying our game build settings. We looked at the Build Settings windows in the last chapter when we set up our scenes for navigation. On the main Unity Editor menu, select File, Build Settings. This will bring up our Build Settings window (Figure 8-1) that shows the multitude of platforms we can build our game for.

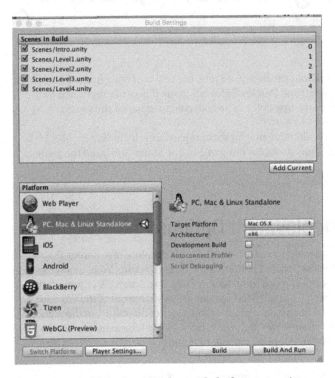

Figure 8-1. *Build Settings Window with deployment options*

Our settings currently have "PC, Mac & Linux Standalone" selected as the platform to build for and is indicated by the Unity icon next to the option. The stand-alone option builds the Unity Game as a non-Web game for the desktop. I'm building my game on a Mac Book Pro but you can choose your platform from the Target Platform drop-down if you are not building for a Mac.

■ **Note**   If the Unity icon is not shown next to the PC, Mac & Linux Standalone option, select the option and click the Switch Platform button. This will change our project to build appropriately.

Clicking on the Player Settings button will reveal the settings we can define for our stand-alone build in the Inspector View of Unity. Here we can change our company name, define our icons, resolution, Splash Image, and other settings of our deployment (Figure 8-2).

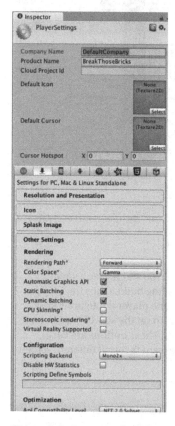

Figure 8-2. *Inspector for PC, Mac & Linux build option*

For now let's leave the default settings and click the Build and Run button on the Build Settings window. This will bring up the Save As display (Figure 8-3) for us to choose a name for the build and save location. Change the game name in the Save As field to "BreakThoseBricks" and click the save button.

Figure 8-3. *Saving the build as a stand-alone desktop game*

This will start the build process and compile the game. You should see a small window appear as the game builds highlighting the steps of the build. Once the generation of the compiled game is complete, the stand-alone player configuration window will appear (Figure 8-4). This window allows for us to set the size of the screen that we are building for and the quality level of the graphics. These options are very helpful if we are building a graphic intensive game that we want to test at different screen sizes and on different PC hardware.

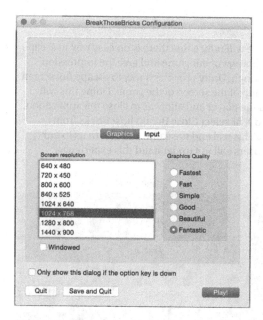

Figure 8-4. *Stand-alone player configuration window*

Our game has simple graphics, so let's launch the game using the default settings. Click the Play button to launch the game. Since we left the defaults, our game was built to run full screen. Therefore our game should launch off the entire screen at the 1024 by 768 resolution. Test out your game by playing the first level.

To view your game file, navigate to the folder where you saved it and search for the application file. Figure 8-5 shows how our application file will look on the Mac. We will set the icons for our game later in the chapter.

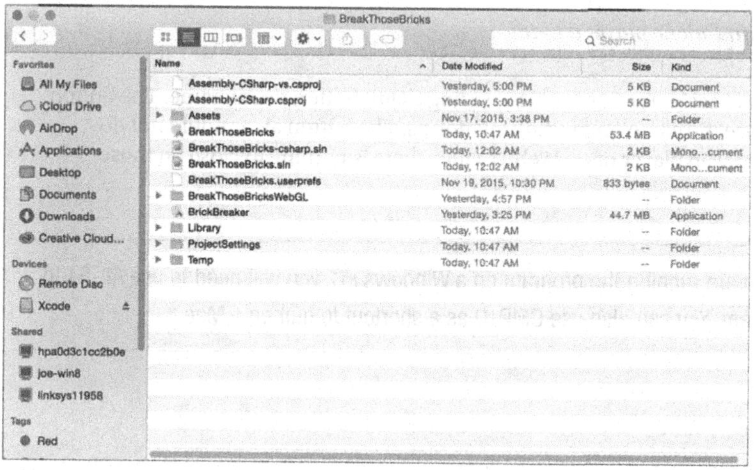

Figure 8-5. *BreakThoseBricks game in the folder of our game*

Adding a Quit Button

Once we are done playing our first level, we will notice that there is no easy way to escape full screen mode. This could confuse the players of our game and give the impression that they cannot exit the game after the launch. Unity provides a way to escape full screen mode by hovering with our mouse at the top of the screen of the game. Doing this will display the window menu of the stand-alone player and allow us to close the application.

To close the application, click the red X or select Close BreakThoseBricks from the BreakThoseBricks menu (Figure 8-6). This will end the game and return us to our desktop. While this may work for us, our users will not understand this experience.

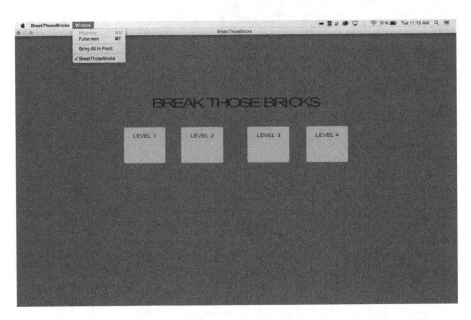

Figure 8-6. Stand-alone player window

Let's make it easier for our users by adding a Quit button to our game. The button will need to close the game on multiple platforms. The button also should not do anything on in a web player or on WebGL since there is nothing to close on those platforms.

> ■ **Note** If you are running the program on a Windows PC, you will need to use Alt-F4 to close the program. You can also use CMD-Q as a shortcut to quit on a Mac

Button Creation and LevelLoader Script Modification

Time to create our new button. We will follow the same steps we used to add the four buttons to our Intro scene in the last chapter. Start by opening the Intro Scene. In the Hierarchy View select the Canvas object. On the main Unity Editor menu, select GameObject, UI, Button. This will add another button to our Canvas that we can manipulate in the Scene View. Select the button and rename it to "Quit Button" in the Inspector View.

Now lets add a Tag to the button. In the Inspector View select the drop-down next to the Tag attribute. Click Add Tag at the bottom of the list and add the "Quit" tag shown in Figure 8-7.

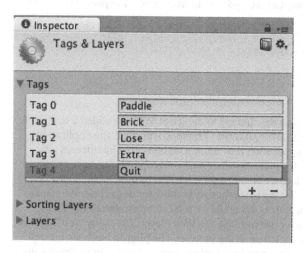

Figure 8-7. Quit Tag added to Quit button on Canvas

This will label our button as Quit in the tagging system and allow for us to reference it in our script. Now let's modify the LevelLoader script that we created in the last chapter. Listing 8-1 shows our modified LevelLoader script:

Listing 8-1. LevelLoader script with QuitGame() method

```
using UnityEngine;
using System.Collections;

public class LevelLoader : MonoBehaviour {
    public GameObject quitButton;

//Basic function for loading level
public void LoadScene (int level)
    {
        Application.LoadLevel(level);
    }
```

```
public void QuitGame(){

    if (Application.isEditor) {
        Debug.Log ("Attempted to quit from the Editor.");
    } else if (Application.isWebPlayer) {
        quitButton = GameObject.FindGameObjectWithTag ("Quit");
        quitButton.SetActive (false);
        Debug.Log ("Attempted to quit from the Web Player.");
    } else if (Application.platform == RuntimePlatform.WebGLPlayer) {
        quitButton = GameObject.FindGameObjectWithTag ("Quit");
        quitButton.SetActive (false);
        Debug.Log ("Attempted to quit from the WebGL Player.");
    }
    else {
        Application.Quit();
    }
  }
}
```

The bold section above contains the changes to the script. We have added a new public method for quitting our application. The QuitGame() method will check the Application runtime data to see what type of application is running. This is very useful since, as was mentioned earlier in the chapter, the platform offers numerous options for deployment.

In our if/then/else condition, we check to see if we are running in the Editor first. If so then the script just prints to the log since there is nothing for us to close. We can use the condition to verify that the button works while we test our app in the Game View.

The second check is to see if we are running in a Web Player. The Unity Web Player is a plug-in that allows for your games to run in the browser. The plug-in has been around for a long time and is very stable. However, one day browsers will stop supporting it since the days of enabling plug-ins in browsers are numbered. For example, Google Chrome no longer supports this plug-in so you people cannot play your game deployed this way on the Chrome browser. If a web player is being used, we just cause our button to disappear.

The third check is to see if the game is running in WebGL. WebGL is the latest web technology that allows us to deploy our game without a plug-in. We will discuss WebGL later in the chapter since we will also build our game in WebGL format. If we are running in WebGL we again cause our button to disappear from the scene.

Finally for any other format we quit the application. With our Quit button finalized, let's build our game for the Web. We will build for WebGL since this is the latest web standard and will not require our players to have a plug-in.

Deploying to WebGL

As I mentioned earlier in the chapter, WebGL is the latest web technology for rendering 3D/2D computer graphics without the need of a browser plug-in. It stands for Web Graphics Library and essentially is a JavaScript API integrated in all standards of the web browser. While most major browsers support WebGL, its availability is dependent on factors external to the browser (like GPU).

Let's build our game for WebGL. Start by changing the build settings for generating a WebGL app. On the main Unity Editor menu, select File, Build Settings. Next select WebGL from the list of platforms available and click the Switch Platform button. This will switch our build generation to WebGL and move the Unity icon next to the selection (Figure 8-8).

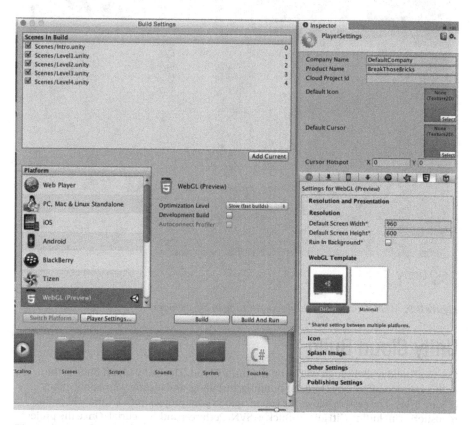

Figure 8-8. *WebGL selected as build platform*

If you click the Player Settings button you will see the setting we can modify for WebGL. Change the Resolution for the Default Screen Width from 960 to 800. This will ensure our game fits the 4:3 resolution we defined for our project. Click the Build and Run button to see our game. You should see the game on the Unity default WebGL template as you see in Figure 8-9. When you click the button to quit the app, it should just disappear from the screen.

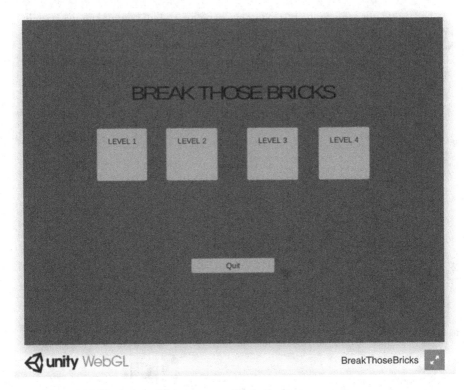

Figure 8-9. WebGL version of the game running in the browser

Unity Cloud Build

Our final build walkthrough will be on the Unity Cloud. The Unity Cloud Build is the online solution offered by Unity for building, installing, and testing your applications (Figure 8-10). The system allows for you to upload your project from a variety of online repositories including GitHub, BitBucket, SVN, Perforce, and Mercurial. Once the project is uploaded, you can build it for numerous platforms simultaneously. This will save you a ton of time since you won't need to continuously switch between the platforms in the Build Settings to deploy your applications.

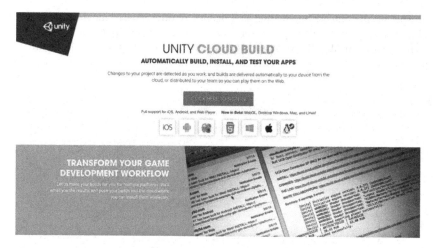

Figure 8-10. *Unity Cloud Build at build.cloud.unity3d.com*

Let's test out our game for Android through the Unity Build Cloud.

Placing Our Game in GitHub

Before we can build our game in the Unity Cloud system we need to have our code in a repository. Since GitHub is a well-known solution and is free, we will use it as the repository of our game. First create an account or log into your existing account in GitHub. Once logged in, click the plus icon on the top right and select "New Repository" from the drop-down.

Figure 8-11. *GitHub account repositories*

149

This will start the process for creating a repository for our game. Name the repository "BreakThoseBricks" and leave it as public for now. Do not select the option to "Initialize this repository with a README." We will add a README file later. Figure 8-12 shows the new repository creation.

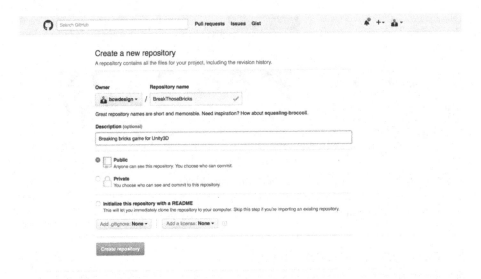

Figure 8-12. *New respository for BreakThoseBricks game*

■ **Note**   Creating your repository as public means that the public can view your project and your code. When you make your game unique you will want to save it to a private repository instead. GitHub charges a fee for saving a repository as private.

Change the description to "Breaking bricks game for Unity3D" and then click the Create Repository button. This will create an empty repository where we can add our files. We will not be able to upload our files from here, however. We will need to install the GitHub desktop app to push the files from our local instance.

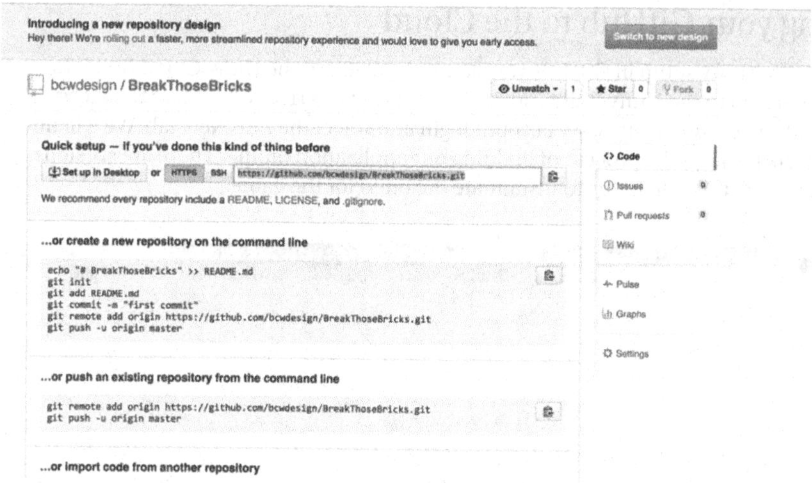

Figure 8-13. New GitHub repository

The details on how to commit files to your repository are displayed on the site. In order to commit the files from your machine you will need to visit https://desktop.github.com and install GitHub locally on your desktop. After the desktop install is complete, visit the command line and navigate to the folder containing the BreakThoseBricks app. Run the commands listed on the site to push your files to GitHub. Your directory should now look like Figure 8-14.

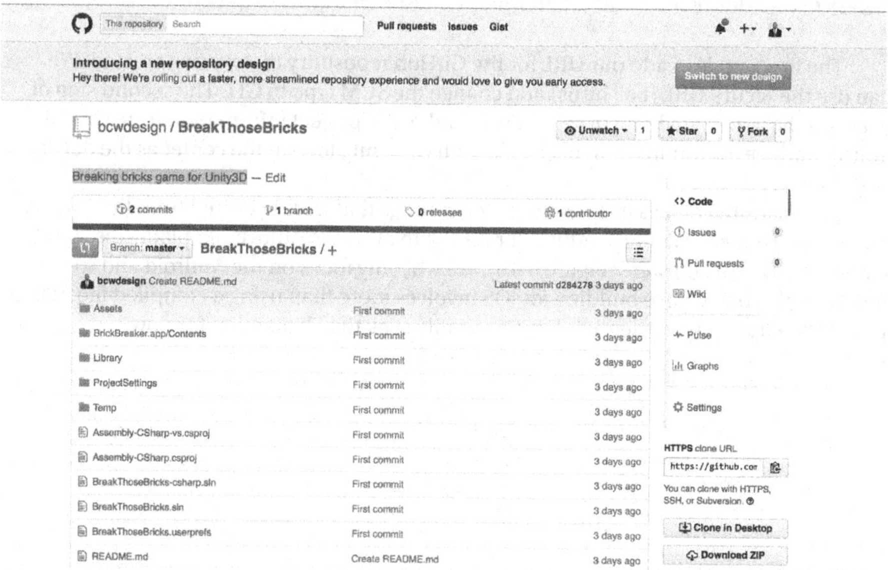

Figure 8-14. Repository with files added

Adding your GitHub to the Cloud

With our repository setup in GitHub, we can now pull it into the Unity Cloud Build. In your browser, go to the Unity Build Cloud site at `https://build.cloud.unity3d.com`. Sign into the site using your Unity account login and select the Add New tab. We will now need to walk through the process of building our application online. There are six steps we need to walk through for us to instantiate the build for the game.

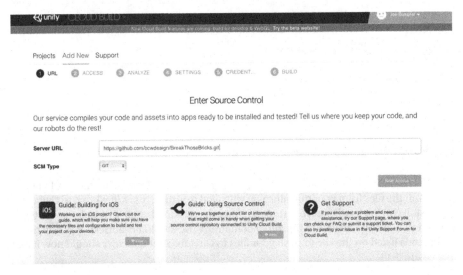

Figure 8-15. *Add New area for Source Control location*

The first step is to add our URL for the GitHub repository that we just created. We can use the secure URL (i.e., https) and change the SCM type to GIT. The second step of access is the automated pull of the Unity Cloud of the project information from GitHub. You should see a spinning icon displayed with the Unity logo in the center as the data is collected.

The third step allows us to evaluate the settings that were acquired from the GitHub repository. Leave the default settings for now with all of the Auto-build platforms selected and the Branch of "master" (Figure 8-16). We will only focus on the Android and web builds for this book since building for iOS involves more than using a compiled file. When you are prompted for credentials for iOS, simply click the Skip option for now.

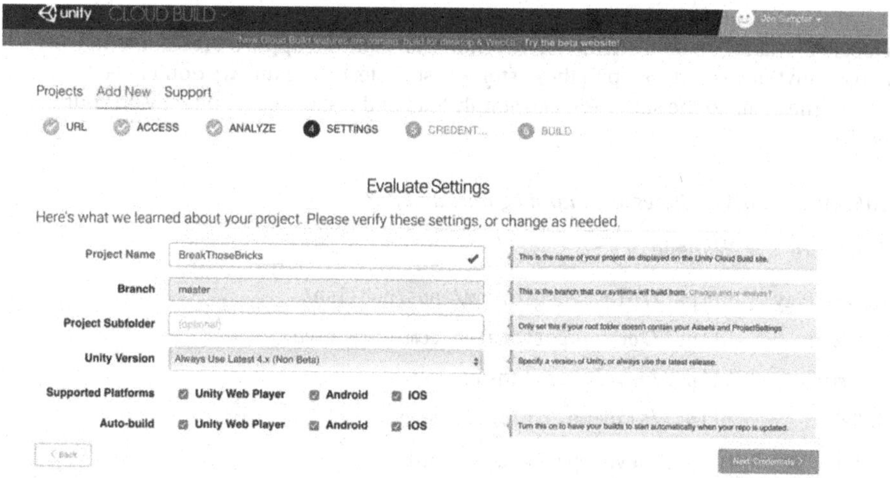

Figure 8-16. Evaluate Settings step for new build

■ **Note**   Due to the extensive details needed to build for iOS, Unity has provided a complete build guide. That guide is located online at `https://build.cloud.unity3d.com/support/guides/ios`

For our Android build we will need to set up the credentials for deploying the game to the store. Enter a Bundle ID that uses the reverse of your domain name along with the game name. My domain is `http://breakthosebricks.com` so my bundle id is set to com.breakthosebricks.BreakThoseBricks. This id must be unique in order to deploy the game to any of the various Android app stores.

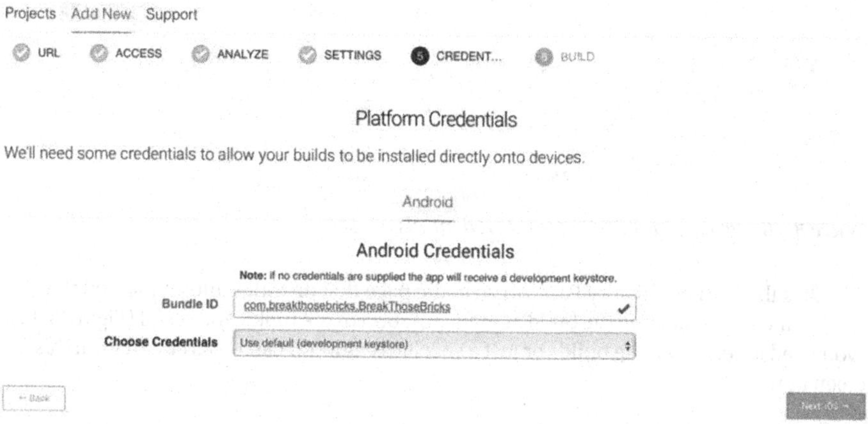

Figure 8-17. Credentials for building for the Android platform

153

Table 8-2 shows a few of the Android app stores available to deploy your game to. Google Play and Amazon are the top two stores for Android apps so I recommend you deploy anything you develop to those stores first. To test our game we don't need to deploy the game to the store. You can simply load and test the game directly on your device.

Table 8-2. Top App Stores for Android games and apps

App Store	Website
Google Play	`https://play.google.com/apps/publish/`
Amazon	`https://developer.amazon.com/home.html`
Samsung	`http://developer.samsung.com/`
SlideME	`http://slideme.org/developers`
GetJar	`http://developer.getjar.mobi`

After your credentials are set for Android, press the Next button and move to the build screen. We will see our project building and have the opportunity to wait for the build to complete (Figure 8-18).

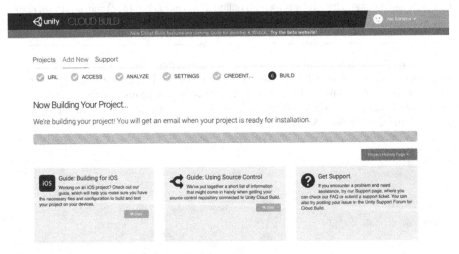

Figure 8-18. Project building after all credentials are set

Click the "Project History Page" to go to the page that provides information on the build. You will see the time the build started, duration of the build, and result (Figure 8-19). If you need to restart all the builds or just a specific build, you can restart them from this screen as well.

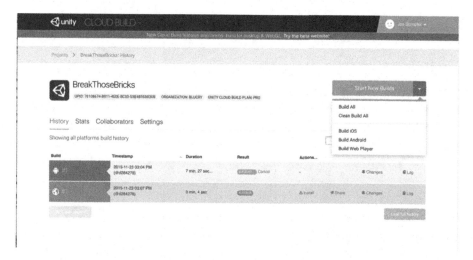

Figure 8-19. *Project History page*

Finally once the build is complete, we can download our Android APK file to our desktop. To load and test the APK on your device you will need to put the file in a place where you can download it to your device. I typically place the file on Google Drive or Dropbox and access the URL to the file from there.

Figure 8-20. *Completed builds with options to download or play*

Summary

In this chapter we compiled our game for various platforms. This included building for desktop, WebGL, and Android. We reviewed building the game locally and in the cloud using the Unity Cloud Build System. Also we discussed using GitHub as our repository for the code files and building our application from it online.

Congratulations, your quest to build a game in a weekend is now complete!

> *A quest is more than a goal. A person sets a goal assuming it is attainable,*
> *but a quest is forbidding, and the prospect of failure is very real.*

—Dr Marcus Ryan, Restless Journey

Index

A

ApplicationLoadLevel()
method, 121
App stores
Build Settings
BreakThoseBricks game, 143
button creation, 145
Inspector View, 141
LevelLoader Script
modification, 145
"PC, Mac & Linux
Standalone", 140
Quit button, 144
Save, 141
stand-alone player configuration
window, 142–143
Unity Game, 140
deployment options, 139–140
Unity Cloud Build *see* (Unity Cloud
Build)
WebGL
build platform, 147
definition, 146
Unity default WebGL
template, 147

B

Background music
"AudioClip" selection, 85
AudioListener, 83, 134
Audio Source, 84, 134
GameManager object, 84
"Loop" check box, 85
"Play on Awake"
check box, 85

C

Classic Arkanoid game, 29
Click() method, 120
Console View, 16
Custom Layout, 17

D

Default layout, 16

E, F

EnableButtons() method, 126

G

Game layout
adding balls, 38
bricks
adding Paddle, 36
camera adjustment, 32
game background, 29
importing assets, 26
PreFab, 33
row of bricks, 35
screen resolution, 28
2D game design setup, 23
Game Manager object and script
case and what decisions, 70
game space, 61
gravity impact, 64
invisible collider walls, 62
lose collider, 71
relabeling game object, 66
UI Text objects, 75
Game View, 14

■ H

Hierarchy View, 13, 17
Hotkeys, 20

■ I, J, K

Inspector View, 15
Integrated development environment
    (IDE) editor, 48

■ L, M, N

launchBall() method, 102
Level manager and menu
    ApplicationLoadLevel() method, 121
    background music, 134
    Build Settings, 130
    EnableButtons() method, 126
    GameManager script
        updation, 122, 126
    Intro scene
        additional buttons, 131
        bricks title text, 117
        buttons, 118
        Canvas option, 116
        Canvas Title object, 117
        Gameobject selection, 116
        Inspector View, 118
        Rect Transform Width
          and Height, 116
        Scene View, 118
        UI Canvas system, 118
    LevelLoader, 119
    LevelManager, 128
    Lose script, 126
    menu screen, 127
    Panel add, 121
    rename and duplicate
        main scene, 128
    restart and main menu buttons, 121
    Trail Renderer, 134
LoadLevel() method, 119
LoadScene() method, 119–120

■ O

OnCollisionEnter2D()
    method, 59, 93, 100, 102
OnPickUp() method, 99, 106
OnTriggerEnter2D() method, 74, 99

■ P

Pause() method, 130
Playmode tint option, 18
Positioning and movement
    ball collisions, 44, 57
    ball friction/bounce, 46
    ball movement, 41
    ball script, 54
    Brick script, with Destroy, 58
    paddle movement, 52
    scripting language
        C Sharp (C#), 48
        editor selection, 48
        first script, 48
Power-ups
    AudioSource, 98
    BasePowerUp object, 97
    bricks rows, 111
    ChangePaddleSize script, 111
    Collider2D, 98
    Extra Balls script
        Ball script modification, 103
        Boolean condition, 102
        launchBall() method, 102
        Paddle, 102–103
        prefab script, 100
        Start() method, 104
        ternary operator, 102
    Growarrow prefab fall, 112
    Lose script, 113
    OnPickUp() method, 99
    OnTriggerEnter2D()
        method, 99
    Paddle size script changes, 105
    Prefab game objects
        Extra Ball, 107
        script list, 106
        shrink and grow prefab
          objects, 108
        sprites, 107
    Prefab scripts, 99
    RigidBody2D, 98
    saving script, 99
    variables, 98
PreFab, 33
Project View, 12–13

■ Q

QuitGame() method, 145

■ R

RequireComponent() function, 86

■ S

Scene View, 14, 17
Sounds
    Brick prefab object, 86
        Brick script modification
            AudioClip object, 90
            Audio Source component, 91
            FallDown variable, 90
            GameManager script, 90
            impact sound play, 87
            minimized brick effect, 91
            variables set, 90
            Woggle animation, 90
        start and end, 85
        walls and paddle, 92
Sprite Editor, 31
Start() method, 50, 104
SwitchState() method, 130

■ T

2D Brick Breaker game, 25

■ U, V

Unity
    computer equipment, 1
    editor and 3D engine, 1
    installation
        component selection window, 4
        configuring Unity, 8
        download introduction window, 3

license management window, 7
    license options, 4
    online Unity account, 6
    Projects window, 7
    Sign-Inwindow, 6
    Unity Download Assistant, 3
    Windows and Mac PCs, 2
    layouts, 16
    runtime background color, 18
    views, 11
Unity Cloud Build
    build.cloud.unity3d.com, 149
    definition, 148
    GitHub
        account creation, 149
        Android APK file, 155
        Android games and apps, 154
        Android platform, 153
        BreakThoseBricks game, 150
        definition, 149
        empty repository, 150
        evaluate settings step, 153
        files, 151
        project building, 154
        Project History Page, 155
        Source Control location, 152
        URL, 152
    project upload, 148
Update() method, 49, 53, 56

■ W, X, Y, Z

WebGL
    build platform, 147
    definition, 146
    Unity default WebGL template, 147
Woggle, 86, 90

Get the eBook for only $5!

Why limit yourself?

Now you can take the weightless companion with you wherever you go and access your content on your PC, phone, tablet, or reader.

Since you've purchased this print book, we're happy to offer you the eBook in all 3 formats for just $5.

Convenient and fully searchable, the PDF version enables you to easily find and copy code—or perform examples by quickly toggling between instructions and applications. The MOBI format is ideal for your Kindle, while the ePUB can be utilized on a variety of mobile devices.

To learn more, go to www.apress.com/companion or contact support@apress.com.

Printed in the United States
By Bookmasters